THE JOURNEY CONTINUES

A sequel to *Apprenticed to a Himalayan Master*

SriM

The Journey Continues

A sequel to *Apprenticed to a Himalayan Master*

Magenta Press

©The Author 2017

First published –April 2017
Second reprint –April 2017
Third reprint- December 2017
Fourth reprint – February 2019

ISBN: 9789382585244
Book Design: J. Menon. www.grantha.com
Typeset: PKS

Printed in India by Manipal Technologies Limited, Manipal

Published by Magenta Press and Publication Pvt. Ltd.,
No.9,1st Floor, Websters Road, Cox Town, Bangalore – 560005, Karnataka,
India Tel: +91 9343071537, info@magentapress.in, www.magentapress.in

My Param Guru Sri Guru Babaji

My Guru Sri Maheshwaranath Babaji

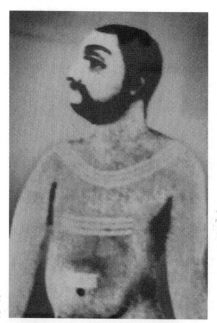

*Sri Sadashiva
Brahmendra*

*Sri Ramakrishna
Paramahamsa*

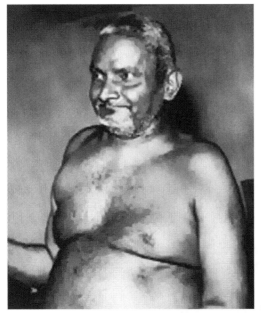

Swami Nityananda

*Swami
Satchidananda*

Contents

Sri M: A Profile

SRI M WAS BORN in Trivandrum Kerala in 1949. At the age of nine he had a strange encounter in the backyard of his house. Under the jackfruit tree he saw a matted-haired yogi. The yogi blessed him saying 'you will get to know our connection in time' and walked away.

After this incident the mind of the young boy, born of Deccani Muslim parents, turned towards Vedanta and the great Indian tradition of yoga that led to deep contemplation. Meeting many known and unknown sages and yogis as if by design, Sri M at the age of 19 left home and went off to the Himalayas. There, at the Vyasa Guha beyond Badrinath, he met the great yogi Sri Maheshwaranath Babaji belonging to the Nath *sampradaya*.

As an apprentice to this great being, his mind underwent a profound transformation. Travelling with this bare-footed yogi, he had many wonderful experiences. A detailed account of his almost unbelievable experiences from childhood to the present can be found in Sri M's autobiography, *Apprenticed to a Himalayan Master: A yogi's Autobiography*.

On the instructions of his master, he returned to the plains and lived incognito for a long time. Meanwhile, he got married and has two children who are themselves grownup and married now.

Sri M wears no grand robes, has no special hair style, is often found wearing jeans and T-shirt or dhothi and white shirt. He lives in Madanapalle, travels around the world conducting retreats and giving talks on yoga, Upanishads, Sufi teachings – in short, inner core of the religious traditions of most religions including the Jewish, the Christian, Buddhist and so on.

He calls himself a practising yogi.

Sri M heads the Satsang Foundation which runs the Satsang Vidyalaya – a free school for the underprivileged and an IIC–ICSC boarding school called Peepal Grove School, a rural school in a remote village 20 kms from Madanapalle and a Swasthya Kendra – a free medical service for the poor.

The Satsang Foundation has recently initiated the MYTHRI programme involving large scale re-forestation and is in the process of setting up a modern hospital to cater to the needy on the outskirts of Bangalore.

Editor

Another Journey Begins

I STARTED MY autobiography *Apprenticed to a Himalayan Master* with the words 'Let the journey begin'. The last chapter was titled 'The journey continues'.

So, completing the autobiography was not the end of the journey and now we begin another journey together into new vistas. A unique and, in many instances, an unbelievably strange journey.

You may dismiss it as fiction or due to my unusually fertile imagination or just plain lies or conclude that I have finally gone bonkers. Be that as it may, if you find the journey interesting and contributing in some way to opening up your mind to newer ways of perception or even bringing up a thought like 'yeah, perhaps there are more unknown vistas to which consciousness can expand than the so-called rational brain can think of', I have done my job.

Bear in mind friends, that the truth is sometimes stranger than fiction and some yogis have even called the solid world we swear by an illusion, a construct of the mind.

There is no strict chronological order though. Each chapter is complete by itself and can be read independently. So dear reader, *Sangacchadvam* – Let's walk together once more.

Sri M

1. Babaji and an Extra-ordinary Photography Session

My guru Maheshwarnath Babaji was not an ordinary man and possessed powers that the average human being cannot comprehend. At twenty and a half years of age, I was aware of that, having spent over a year wandering with him in the Himalayas. The more I watched him at close quarters, the more I marvelled at the wisdom and superhuman capacities of this enigma in human form. Whenever asked, he always said, "There are no miracles. Many laws of nature are still unknown to most of humanity. When someone who knows these laws operates them, and does something, then those who don't know think they are witnessing a miracle." *Shon* ✶

I shall now relate one such instance and pen down the deeply significant dialogue that followed the event.

* * * * *

I had been living with Babaji for over a year. We were staying in Rishikesh, on the other side of the Ganga, in a solitary cave. As you walk across the present Ram Jhula and cross the Ganga, the path towards the left leads to Laxman Jhula, and the one on the right, after passing through the bazaar and crossing Gita Bhavan and Parmarth Niketan on the left, continues to a wooded area. Turn left and you enter the forest that leads to Mouni Baba's cave and beyond to Neelkanth. Further, on the right, on the banks of the Ganga are two caves.

At the time that I am speaking of, most of the ashrams were small and the bazaar not as noisy and dirty as it is now. There were very few shops. All that changed with the arrival of the Beatles, for whom Maharishi Mahesh Yogi built air-conditioned caves to meditate in, and later the turning of Rishikesh into a weekend picnic spot for tourists, leaving the *Dev Bhoomi* strewn with plastic and plastered with blatant consumerism. In those days, when it was mainly a retreat for *sadhus*, you could find solitude even during the pilgrim season when a lot of people came to visit Badri, Kedar, Gangotri and Yamunotri.

The caves I mentioned, tucked away in a remote corner on the banks of the great river, were ideal for the serious seeker. You can still see them. Recently, on my last visit, I saw that one of them had been whitewashed, fitted with a green metal door and was occupied by a handicapped, ex-service man, who told me that he was fed up with life.

Babaji and I lived in this cave off and on. It was our practice to take a boat and cross to the other side in the evenings, to sit at the quiet ghat near the *kutir* of Swami Sivananda of the Divine Life Society and talk of various things until the lamps were lit and the *aarti* was performed to the holy river.

Babaji had an aversion to being photographed. In fact, knowing that I was an artist myself, he had prohibited me from drawing or painting his portrait. Though prohibited, I

2

was still rebellious, and thought that I could get his photograph somehow, even if he did not want one taken. I had not yet, fully understood that if he did not wish something to happen, it would not, no matter how much I, in my foolishness and ignorance, however well-meaning, wanted it to happen.

So one evening, I secretly arranged for a photographer to come to the ghat, where Babaji and I would be either meditating or engaged in a dialogue. I had befriended a photographer, a young Gharwali from Dehradun named Prashanth Rawat. Several days ago, we had agreed that he would come around 5 pm to the Sivananda ghat on a certain day. He was to pretend to be a stranger, a tourist, casually click a photograph of Babaji and disappear quietly. He said he was going to Dehradun, but would travel back to Rishikesh on the appointed day and do the needful. He was as eager to get Babaji's picture as I was and took it as a challenge.

On that particular evening, my only fear was that Babaji would cancel the walk. He did not. "Madhu, let's cross to the other side and sit on the steps of the Sivananda ghat, your favourite spot," he said. So, we sat on the steps facing the river and Babaji, reminisced about old Rishikesh, when there were no big ashrams, except the Swarg Ashram.

"Swami Sivananda had not as yet founded the Divine Life Society and lived in a small *kutir*, on the other side, belonging to the Swarg Ashram. People called him 'Doctor *Swami*' because he treated sick sadhus."

I asked him a few questions about Laxman Jhula and *Purani Jhadi* and he answered them. Then, the discussion went on to certain personal matters regarding sadhana. I was becoming a little restless and anxious as there was no sign of Rawat, the photographer. One hour passed and still no Rawat in sight. Finally, Babaji looked into my eyes and said in a matter-of-fact way, "No point in getting distracted and restless Madhu, that photographer of yours won't come."

I was stunned. "Babaji, I... Babaji, I am sorry. I will never again commit such a mistake. You know my thoughts even before I start thinking them. Please forgive me... I am...." I burst into tears.

Babaji patted my back. "It's all right," he said, "control yourself. Not a big crime and you learnt a good lesson anyway."

"Come, let's go back before it gets too dark."

Soon, we were sitting in front of the cave facing the Ganga. The sun had painted the sky a beautiful pink. "Now," said Babaji, "Do you think that your photographer could have taken a picture without my concurrence? No, and I'll tell you why. Look at me now."

I shifted my gaze from the flowing waters and looked in his direction.

"Oh!" I exclaimed loudly, surprised by what I saw. Instead of his body, all I could see was a grey, translucent silhouette.

Babaji's voice which now came from the shadowy outline continued. "How do you see an object? Light falls on an object and its reflected rays fall on the lens of your eyeballs and an image is formed. It's the same for a camera. The light is reflected onto the camera lens and the image falls on the film."

"Well, what if we know how to prevent the light rays from reflecting back and instead absorb them into our bodies? A powerful mind tuned to the stillness of the Supreme Self, the core of our consciousness can control the light rays, absorb them and not let them reflect. You would then see only a grey, translucent outline and not the body you are familiar with. Under dimly lit conditions, you would not even see the outline."

"That's exactly what I am doing now. Not letting the light rays reflect. The camera would not have captured the image, if I so desired."

I said, "Got the message, Babaji, please reappear in the form I love to see."

In an instant, he was back in his usual form.

"So," I asked, "is this how yogis disappear?"

"Mostly," said Babaji "but there is one more method where one actually disintegrates the primary particles of the body temporarily, but only most advanced yogis can do that."

"Please, can you explain Babaji?"

"The primary particles that make up both animate and inanimate matter are called quarks. Quantum physics, having demolished the absolute certainty of Newtonian physics, is now faced with an enigma called the Theory of Uncertainty. The primary substance that goes to form matter cannot now be pronounced with certainty, to be either particles or waves."

"Strangely, when observed they tend to shift from particles to waves and vice versa. When they are observed behaving like particles, they suddenly start behaving like waves. Some physicists even advance the theory that their behaviour depends on the observer."

"However, the great *Rishis* hold that consciousness is the primary core of all existence and that at the deepest level, it can change particles to waves or waves to particles at will. A completely tranquil mind, which the *Vajrayāna Buddhists* call the vacuous mind, is in tune with this core of all existence. A yogi, established in that state, can change the particles of his body to waves which become invisible to the organs of perception like the eyes etc. The yogi can then travel to other locations and convert back into visible particle based forms."

"This is not easy and only great beings like Sri Guru Babaji can practise this kind of disintegration and reintegration. To put it simply, dissolution of the body into its primary elements and re-gathering them at will to form the body again. Nothing to do with optical illusions performed on stage by illusionists."

"Babaji, can I also learn to do this?"

Babaji laughed. "You have to go a long way, my son. Do your *kriya* and meditate for some time before the reality of hunger begins to gnaw at your insides."

We sat together, still facing the great river, and went into deep meditation until darkness fell all around us, but we were absorbed in the inner light that is self-illumined and blissful.

Two days later, I sought out my friend, the photographer at Laxman Jhula to find out what had happened.

"I think your Guru prevented me from coming," said Rawat. "I got into a bus at Dehradun well in time and halfway through, the front tyre got punctured. I had to wait for another bus. Half an hour after I got into the second bus, there was a grating sound. The driver said that he would have to stop because there was something wrong with the clutch or gear or something."

"I was already late but I managed to persuade a cab driver, who was on his way to Rishikesh to take me along. Can you believe it? The rear tyre of the cab got punctured! By then it was dark and I decided to give up and go back to Dehradun. I came back the next day, and everything went fine. But, I wouldn't mind taking another chance."

"Forget it," I said. "It won't work."

* * * * *

I gave up the idea of having Babaji photographed, and said to myself, that some day, I would paint or draw his portrait, until one morning when Babaji said, "You are also not supposed to paint or draw my portrait." That clinched the issue then, but many years after his *Mahasamadhi*, I did attempt once again to paint his likeliness.

That's another story and I will tell you what happened.

Many years after Babaji's passing away, having settled in Madanapalle and leading a semi-bachelor's life, considering that my wife and kids were in Rishi Valley where my wife was teaching, it occurred to me one morning that I should once again attempt to draw a portrait of Babaji.

I justified my intention by saying to myself that the stricture against painting his picture was laid by him many years ago, and had probably expired by now. In any case, if he did not wish it to happen, it would not, but there was no harm in trying. Babaji, who was fond of quoting Jesus who said, 'the law was made for man, not man for the law', would probably appreciate my deep longing to show his form to those of my friends to whom I had spoken so passionately about him.

So, on that hot summer morning, I fixed a sheet of paper to the drawing board, armed myself with a couple of brushes and directly, in my minimum strokes style, painted a really good portrait of Babaji in black ink. By then, it was twelve O'clock. I leaned the board against the wall of the open verandah of my house, so that it would dry well, and came in to have an early lunch. I was quite satisfied and delighted with my work.

After lunch, I went upstairs to the bedroom to take a quick siesta. I must tell you that when I went to sleep, the sky was absolutely clear and blue, with not a cloud in sight. I must have slept for about an hour or so, when I was woken up by a loud thunder clap. I thought I was dreaming because it never rains in Madanapalle in May. But it was raining copiously.

It was then that I remembered the picture in the verandah. Rushing down the stairs, I ran outside and was heartbroken! The rain had washed away the picture, except for an uneven outline and the paper itself was soaked thoroughly. I could do nothing, the picture was lost. In ten minutes flat, the rain ceased, the clouds vanished and the sky was as blue as before. I knew then, that the stricture against painting or drawing his picture was still in force and it would be foolish to attempt it again. So it stayed, till I wrote my autobiography many years later.

* * * * *

The picture you will find in this book and also in the autobiography came to be drawn this way.

Having written the autobiography, which Babaji himself had ordered me just before he passed away to write it 'at the right time', I was wondering what to do. It would be unfair to the readers to not carry Babaji's picture in the book. I waited for a sign, a dream or vision or something to give me a green signal. None came, but then, the eternal rebel that I am, I decided to give it another try.

I sat down one morning in my study and made a pencil sketch of Babaji. It was okay but I was not satisfied. The next day, I had to go to the Peepal Grove School, the boarding school run by the Satsang Foundation. There, I gave the sketch to the art teacher Mr. Sharat and asked him to work on it, after he copied it to his laptop. After many alterations and corrections, a final picture emerged, with which I was satisfied. A print out was taken and I carried it in a file carefully. It was sacred to me.

Every day, I looked at it to be sure that it had not disappeared. Even when it was with the printer, I kept my fingers crossed. When the picture appeared in the first copy of the autobiography, I sighed with relief. Babaji had allowed me to publish it in his infinite kindness and perhaps love for the readers.

The day after the book was out, I dreamt of Babaji after a long time. He smiled and said, "You have done it Madhu," and floated away into the clouds.

2. Nityananda of Ganesh Puri and the Hard Slap

Many years ago there lived a man in Ganeshpuri, not far from Mumbai, who was considered a great saint by thousands of his followers, inspite of his eccentric ways and often, crazy behaviour. Nityananda was his name.

You will find his picture in my autobiography but if you have read it, you may have wondered why nothing is written about him. I shall now tell you why the chapter about him was not included in the autobiography, and also my strange encounter with him at the age of twelve. It took me eight years after the incident to understand the deep significance of the hard and painful slap he gave me on my right cheek the moment he laid eyes on me.

First, let me state the reason why nothing was written in my autobiography although his picture was printed.

Chronologically, my meeting with Nityananda was to be included among the chapters of my early life, but try as I might, every time I sat down to write, nothing would come into my head. It was as if my brain had been wiped clean, except for his form which kept appearing and disappearing. Taking that as a sign that I was to try later, I wrote the rest of the chapters. The entire manuscript was complete and I tried again, but to no avail.

One day while meditating, it occurred to me that perhaps Nityananda did not want me to write anything about him, may be not at that time. So I sent the manuscript away to the editor and forgot that his photograph had already been included. There were no queries about this from the editor either and finally the book was out.

A year later, whilst sitting on the verandah of my jungle retreat 'Hill View' adjoining the Rajiv Gandhi National Park at Bandipur gazing at the blue Nilgiri Hills in the distance, the whole story came back to me in a flash and has remained with me ever since.

* * * * *

Here is the story:

On my mother's side of the family, there were a number of eccentrics but on my paternal side there was only one man who could be called rather strange and very different from the rest of the family (who though not being ultra-orthodox, followed the tenets of Islam). He was Abdul Aziz, head master of the local school, called Ajji Bhai by his relatives and Ajji Mian Sir by his students. He was my father's first cousin – his father's sister's son – but much older than my father.

He was a confirmed bachelor, which by itself was frowned upon by Islam. To make matters worse, he never went to the mosque or performed the ritual of Islamic prayer called *namaz*. He read the Hindu scriptures, practised yoga and was an expert in the Japanese arts of self-defence like judo and ju-jitsu, which he had picked up while studying at the

American College, Madurai, a prestigious institution in those days. It was from him that I first heard the word *Kundalini*.

I remember him as a tall and well-built old man with closely cropped silver hair and a white, clipped moustache, which made his stern face even sterner. Clad in his khaki half-sleeved shirt and a white *mundu* (ankle length sarong), he looked like a retired soldier or policeman who had returned to his home town after fighting many a battle. Not that he shied away from a fight even then. Quick to anger, he was ready for combat at the slightest provocation and I had seen him handle a drunk, using an umbrella as his weapon.

Once every two months or so he would come to visit us from his home town Punalur, forty miles away, and stay for a few days. I always looked forward to his visits for many reasons. He taught me ju-jitsu and judo; he loved to see me practise my *asanas* and *Kalaripayattu*. He read out the adventures of Sherlock Holmes to me and discussed the art of detection. He told me fascinating stories of yogis, one of whom had a manuscript written on human skin, which taught the science of *kaya kalpa* or rejuvenation and about a mysterious power called the *Kundalini*, which transformed man to super-man and such occult subjects.

Although my father dismissed most of them as tall stories, he dared not say that to him directly, for one he was much older, somewhat of a father figure and the head master of the school he had studied in.

One morning after a sumptuous breakfast, while he sat on the easy chair smoking a cheroot, Ajji Bhai gestured to me to come closer. Inspite of the terrible odour of the cheroot I went and sat next to him, eager to hear his stories.

"Are you prepared for an adventure?" he whispered. "If you are, I can take you to see Swami Nityananda, a mysterious yogi with supernatural powers. But it has to be totally confidential, only between you and me."

"Yes," I said fascinated, "but how?"

"I am going to tell your father, that I am taking you to my friend Mulluvillai's rubber estate in Edamon near Punalur for a few days to teach you judo and coach you in Math. I think he won't object. Do you think you can stay away from your mother for a few days?"

"Yes," I said.

So the conspiracy was hatched and as there were no cell phones and the land lines never worked properly, our secret was kept.

To cut a long story short, we travelled for four days – by train to Chennai, then Mumbai and finally by bus from Mumbai to Ganeshpuri. We reached Ganeshpuri around 11 am and went straight to Nityananda's abode, which was called 'Kailash'. By then I was tired as I had not slept well, hungry, had a slight headache and was feeling very home sick since this was the first time I was travelling without my family. We were told to wait in a queue. There were at least fifty people waiting to have *darshan* of the saint. In half an hour, a gate was opened and we were ushered in.

On an easy chair sat a rather frightening figure. He was huge with a shiny, black complexion and a shaven head and face that seemed strangely small compared to the rest of his body, especially his tight protruding belly. All he wore was a small, white loin cloth and was bare foot. I was scared, for apart from his formidable physique he seemed crazy. He was muttering to himself in some incoherent language, making strange gestures with his hands and now and then breaking into chuckles for no apparent reason.

The line of devotees walked past him. When they came face to face, they prostrated, sought his blessings and moved on. He touched some on their heads, others he just waved away and in one case, he shouted loudly. For a second, it seemed he was going to assault him, but the moment passed and the next in line, stepped forward.

By the time our chance came, I was shivering with fear, though my uncle held my hand. Standing in front of Nityananda who now seemed to me like a huge mountain, I imitated the other devotees and prostrated. When I raised my head, stood up and looked at his face, all fear vanished. He smiled sweetly, a motherly smile, full of affection and patted my head muttering in *Malayalam*. The only words I could catch were, "*Mala Kaeranum*" (will have to climb mountains), and something that sounded like "*thorakkum, thorakkum, thorakkum pinnae*" (must open, must open, must open later on).

When my uncle said to him in *Malayalam* that he did not understand what he was saying, he got angry and shouted at him to get out and get lost. Still angry, he glared at me and then he suddenly slapped me hard on my right cheek. The slap was so powerful that I fell down on my side. The cheek felt like it was on fire. I burst into tears, wailed loudly, as I picked myself up. My uncle quietly led me out, consoling me saying "It is your good luck. That was a blessing. Few people get such a blessing. Don't worry."

I dried my tears with my handkerchief, but did not agree with him. What kind of blessing was that, slapping an innocent nine year old? I was convinced that the saint was completely mad and that this whole journey was a misadventure. We had a quick lunch in a hotel and left immediately. I hardly spoke to Ajji Bhai on the journey back, which again took tiring four days.

We returned to Trivandrum and no one asked any uncomfortable questions. I lied to my parents and said I had learnt more judo and a little mathematics. My uncle returned to Punalur. His parting words were, "I don't know what the significance of that slap was, but I think you will discover the reason sometime later in your life."

* * * * *

I continued to think of the incident as the mad outburst of a mentally deranged person until the age of sixteen or so, when I came to understand that certain highly evolved sages called *avadhutas* sometimes behaved in strange ways to achieve objectives not known to us ordinary mortals. Perhaps there was some significance to the slap, I thought, but what it actually was I found out many years later when I had run away from home and had been accepted as Babaji's apprentice.

Whilst living in the *Charan Paduka* cave in Badrinath, Babaji taught me a certain breathing technique which was aimed at clearing the *ida nadi*, the pathway through which life energy or *prana* courses through the left side of the body. I practised it to perfection and Babaji was convinced that the *ida nadi* pathway had been cleared totally. When I asked him if I had to do the same for the right side, which is called the *pingala nadi*, he laughed and said, "That was done long ago by Nityananda's slap on your right cheek. It's clean and clear now and you don't have to worry about it. I know you thought he was mad!"

Strange are the ways of sages and saints, very often beyond the understanding of our little brains.

3. He Loved Wild Elephants Too

From my friend Jerry Jones's living room in Portland, Oregon, I can see the snow covered Mount Hood. I have always loved the mountains, big or small – the great Himalayan range, the Karokoram, Mount Kailash called *Kang Rinpoche* (precious jewel) by the Tibetans, the Andes in Chile, the Western Ghats in South India, even the hills of black granite that rise not far away from my residence in Madanapalle, Andhra Pradesh, lesser known cousins of the great mountain Tirumalai, older than the Himalayas according to geologists, on which stands the famous temple of Lord Venkateshwara.

Man has been fascinated with mountains from time immemorial and there are mountaineers who try and scale peaks such as Mt. Everest and other high ranges risking their very lives. Some die and some bask in the glory of having conquered the unconquerable. What is it that fascinates us, when we look at the mountains or the deep, dark woods or the flowing rivers, the murmuring brooks, the bright flowers and colourful butterflies, even the toothless, wide eyed innocent smile of an infant? Why do we feel so tranquil, watching a quiet sunset on the seashore or feel so thrilled to be woken up by a bird song or see a blue kingfisher flash past the window? Have you come close to an elephant in the wild or seen a tiger in the jungle licking its paws? I have, and the feeling of awe and wonderment that grips the mind overcomes any fear.

Years ago, as I wandered in the Himalayas, I pondered over this. I also discussed this with Maheshwarnath Babaji. I would like to share my thoughts with you on this subject and end with a story of Babaji and the wild elephant.

Anything designed by the human mind is indeed conditioned and corrupted by the limitations of thought. The brain is still limited despite its ability to expand its horizons. Pure nature is not man made and the closer you are to it, the quieter becomes the mind. Perhaps, closeness to nature, eventually 'de-conditions' the mind and one is in touch with the infinite being, the Source and reality untouched by limiting concepts and conditioned responses of thought.

Deep down, in the inner recesses of the psyche, there is this innate longing to shed this conditioning and return to the purity and infinitude which is its original source. Mountains, rivers, deserts, forests, all those not made by man, evoke this longing and in some way take one closer to that original unconditional Being. Once, as I looked at the distant peaks of the snow-clad Daulagiri range, something snapped in my heart and 'I' no longer existed. There is only the mountain. I stood towering, a pure white being, looking compassionately down at the world, that stretched before me.

The desire to climb, conquer, expand and so on is again an expression of man's desire to reach that state of completeness called *Purna* in the scriptures. But, sadly one is never complete and finally is laid to rest or reduced to ashes – *bhasmantam shareeram*. 'For dust thou art, and unto dust shalt thou return'[1]. In the quietness of natural contemplation, as you watch the river wind its way down the valley or the simple white cloud resting on the tip of a dark cliff or the majestic flash of silver streaks of lightning against the night sky, this completeness steals in silently. You cannot force it to come. It comes uninvited and when it does, you cannot hold it back. 'Let go and rejoice' says the *Isavasya Upanishad*. Sheer effortlessness heralds its arrival, like a gentle, fragrant breeze. It is what it is. No words can describe it.

When man interferes with nature, when concrete monstrosities are built across the mighty flowing rivers, damning (and damming) their free movement, curtailing their natural freedom, disasters are around the corner. Nature in its fury destroys, so that a new order is established. A river finds its own embankment. To understand nature is not to interfere with it but to curtail our immense greed and come to terms with nature.

* * * * *

Here is a true story to show you how even wild animals recognise a specially evolved being who has touched the ultimate source and lives as one with nature. In those days, Maheshwarnath Babaji and I lived in Mouni Baba's cave, which is in the middle of the forest between Rishikesh and Neelkant Mahadev. The forest was then thicker than it is

---

1 Genesis 3:19

now and leopards and elephants roamed freely especially at night. Sadhus and pilgrims who occasionally frequented the locality, carried drums and gongs to frighten the animals and avoided travelling at night. I had seen elephants walk past as I sat near the mouth of the cave but never once did they come close or behave destructively.

One day, three *Bairagi* sadhus came to meet Babaji. A rogue elephant was behaving violently and had turned terribly destructive, they said. It had killed at least six people, including two forest guards. The forest department was at its wit's end and was unable to capture it. Only the day before, they said, it had raided a sadhu's *kutir* and trampled him to death. People were afraid of travelling to Neelkant because the elephant lurked, hidden in the forest midway between Rishikesh and Neelkant, not far from Mouni Baba's cave. It would even attack in broad day and could Babaji help in some way?

Babaji smiled and said, "Today, I shall not do anything about the elephant God who is angry. Tomorrow, being the full moon, I shall see what I can do. Meanwhile, please stay here tonight and have no fear. *Hari Om*." With that the conversation ended and Babaji turned to me and said, "Tomorrow night, come with me. We need to teach *Gajnath* a good lesson and calm him down."

Around midnight Babaji woke me. The full moon was out in all its glory. We walked down from the cave and entered the forest. We walked for a while and then sat down on a flat surfaced rock. After a while, I saw a full grown leopard come out of the bushes in front of us. It looked in our direction and stopped.

Babaji said, "Put your palms together in *namaskar* and bow to the leopard. Say in your mind, you are a manifestation of the Divine, you are the companion of Durga. We mean no harm. I bow before you." I did as instructed. The leopard stared at us for a long time and then walked away.

We waited for the elephant. He appeared suddenly from nowhere and burst forth from behind us. He trumpeted and charged towards us. Babaji and I turned around. I froze with fear. Just before he reached us, Babaji put up his right hand and the elephant froze. It stood still and looked at Babaji with complete attention, with one of his front legs lifted up and moving his body back and forth with his three legs in a swaying motion.

Babaji spoke to him firmly but softly in Hindi. I know this sounds insane but I shall not desist from reporting the incident. "So," said Babaji, "is this the way to behave dear friend? I know you resent the presence of noisy human beings who disturb your solitude but this is no way to react. You are in the state of *mast*. I can see it. The excess male hormones are influencing your actions. I'll make all that subside and you will soon become normal. Here!"

Before my astonished eyes, Babaji stepped forward and placed his right hand on the elephant's forehead. With the left, he stroked his trunk. The elephant stopped swaying, went down on his knees and touched Babaji's feet with the tip of his trunk. He then stood up and raising his trunk high up, trumpeted with joy and moved away. He gave up his violent behaviour and thereafter it was safe for pilgrims and sadhus to move freely.

Later, when I heard a similar story about the inimitable Akkalkot ka Maharaj, Swami Samarth, I had no difficulty believing it. It is said that the great Swami tamed an elephant who had gone *mast*, and was wreaking havoc by walking up to him and landing a hard slap on his cheek, saying 'behave yourself'.

* * * * *

Before I end, a note of warning. Do not hypnotise yourself into believing that you are a highly evolved yogi or spiritual being and try taming wild animals. The results would most likely be disastrous. There was this young sanyasin who went to perform austerities in the Kodachadri peak, close to the famous Mookambika Devi temple in Kollur. He was warned that a leopard was frequenting the cave, but he took no heed. He had heard of the tiger which used to come to the Virupaksha cave where the great Sri Ramana Maharishi meditated, and who is said to have petted the tiger according to an old lady who witnessed the act from afar.

The young monk tried to attempt the same feat when the leopard appeared, but was unfortunately torn to pieces. They found his mutilated body after many days. So watch out. Not everyone is highly evolved spiritually. Steer clear of wild animals. If you don't disturb them they generally leave you alone. In any case, don't walk up to a wild elephant and transmit loving thoughts. It will most likely not work.

4. The Great Dream

I am not much of a dreamer. Like everybody else, I have had several dreams mostly short ones of no significance whatsoever, but three times in my life, I have had dreams, long and involved ones which I am hesitant to call random and insignificant. Of those three dreams, the one which I have written about in my autobiography came as an indication that it was time to start teaching in public. The one which I am now going to relate has to do with my past lives and was like a replay of what happened.

* * * * *

The dream begins in Pataliputra, now Patna in Bihar, which was then a thriving, bustling port and cosmopolitan city. I was an extremely rich merchant named Dhana and lived a life of pleasure seeking and extravagance. I had built my fortune through hard work (or so I thought), from a poor menial labourer to a merchant with several caravans.

My treasury was filled with gold and precious jewels which even a king would envy. In my harem were beautiful courtesans who could give me all the pleasures of the world. Leading a life of extreme indulgence and drunken orgies, I lost all touch with simple realities of life. The only thing that I was interested in was to increase my wealth further, for I believed that wealth was the key to happiness.

I continued on this path until one day, destiny dealt a deadly blow that shattered my life and blew the certainty in my life to bits. First, my wife ran away with my best friend who was a poor artisan. She felt I was more in love with my wealth and my indulgences than with her. Soon my son and daughter, whom I adored, abandoned me and went away with their mother. For sometime, I tried to disguise my grief and cover it up with more lustful excesses, till it struck me one day, that the entire foundation of the philosophy of my life that wealth produced happiness had received a deathly blow and had been shattered to pieces.

Distraught and not knowing where to turn, I was sitting near the Ganga one evening, miserable and shaken, even contemplating suicide, when I saw a number of wandering naked asetics called *digambaras*, sitting on the nearby ghats and meditating. Their faces reflected a tranquillity and simplicity that I found quite attractive. That set me thinking. Does abandoning wealth and even the loin cloth, bring happiness? Does renunciation bring peace?

I moved closer and sat near them. After a long meditation, they opened their eyes and talked in low, gentle tones. One of them, who seemed to be the leader said, "Now, O *parivrajakas*, we should head towards a place close to Rajgriha. It seems a great teacher who has reached the highest state of spiritual fulfilment is camping there for a few days and giving his sermons. An elderly, learned *digambara*, I know for several years said to me that this great being, who was a prince before he became a wandering ascetic, is the teacher of the age, a *tirthankara*. The learned *digambara* has already walked towards this place to listen to the sermons."

"Let's hasten towards Rajgriha and have a glimpse of the *tirthankara* and hear his words. Perhaps, we shall find the bliss of total and final freedom that we have been seeking for so long."

Something stirred in the deepest recesses of my mind. I still had lots of wealth. Here was a chance to see the great One. I negotiated with the monks. There was a long distance to travel and I would look after all their needs, if they would let me travel with them. So I placed a caravan at their disposal. It carried food and gold coins and with four assistants and guards, I travelled with the monks.

The journey was difficult for me, for the *sramanas* walked barefoot through sometimes treacherous terrain and I dressed simply in a loin cloth and upper garment walked with them. After many days of this torturous journey for me – as the *sramanas* were well composed and showed no sign of distress – we reached a place not very far from Rajgriha. There I saw a wonderous sight.

There sat an elegant and handsome man with a royal demeanour, completely naked. He sat cross-legged under an Asoka tree. The place surrounded by forests was beautiful and the lion like man who was the central figure, was beautiful too. The *sramanas* bowed and sat down. Many renunciants and householders sat in front of him, in semi circles. Merchants, monks, kings and princes, men and women, young and old, dogs and deer sat before him. There was complete silence.

The great one's eyes were half open. There was stillness in the air. Not a single leaf moved. Soulful silence prevailed and then from his sacred presence emanated a divine sound, which I could compare to nothing. It was a deep reverberation, sweet, tranquil and peaceful. No words were said but the voice of silence conveyed all that was to be conveyed.

This is what I understood: "To all beings, life is dear. All living beings seek happiness. Hurt not any living beings. Do not kill any living beings. Non-violence is the highest of qualities. Live a life of restraint. Lead a simple life and do not stray from truth into falsehood. Appreciate everyone's point of view for the truth is multi-dimensional. Renounce ego and be free. Beyond this perishable body and the world around, is your immortal soul, which in its pure state is divine."

"All this you have understood theoretically. Now practice the way of life till you realise this actually. The journey is long. It will take you several lives but walk on the path through travails and turmoil until you become a winner, a free and blissful soul."

Sublime peace entered my heart and I bowed down in reverence.

*****

The next minute I woke up and wished the dream had not ended; a long dream which had indicated a forgotten facet of my past lives. I washed my face and went to the office of the Krishnamurti Foundation headquarters at Vasant

Vihar in Chennai. I was a resident there. J. Krishnamurti had arrived for the annual talks and there was much work to do.

Many times I thought of discussing the dream with J. Krishnamurti, but could never bring myself to. On the day of his departure, I had gone to his room to see if everything was in order, when he literally shocked me by holding my arm and saying, "Don't talk to anyone about the dream. Not yet. Keep it to yourself."

I think it is now time to divulge the secret dream.

5. My Darshan of Guruvayurappan

Now I am going to tell you about one of the most soul-stirring and mind transforming experiences of my life. This happened in the famous temple of Guruvayur, where the prankish heart stealer god Krishna is worshipped as a young boy. I had guarded this blissful experience in the secret recesses of my heart until now, and perhaps related it only to a few good friends. One of them, a close friend and a communist at heart, called it my 'most touching hallucination', but that is his opinion and he is entitled to it. Each person is free to choose what he or she believes in.

Be that as it may, I think it is time now to share this extraordinary experience of mine with you. This is all the more significant as I was not born a Hindu and Guruvayur is one of the few temples where even today non-Hindus are not allowed entry. There must be reasons why this rule was promulgated in the olden days and we shall not go into such matters here. I write as a lover of Krishna – nothing more or less!

While many may not have heard of the Guruvayur temple, in the south of India especially in Kerala and Tamil Nadu, it is one of the most well-known temples of Krishna, perhaps even more popular than the Sri Anantha Padamanabha Swami temple of Travancore, where I was born.

For those who may not be familiar, it would be in order I think, to provide a brief introduction to Guruvayur.

Legends have it that the deity is five thousand years old, although there are no historical records. The story goes that the idol, carved out of a sacred material called *Pathalanjana Sila*, was once worshipped by the great God Maha Vishnu and handed over to Brahma. After many generations, it was worshipped by Sri Krishna's parents Vasudeva and Devaki, and later installed in Dwaraka and worshipped by Krishna himself.

Before giving up his body, Krishna handed over this idol to his foremost disciple, Uddhava and instructed him to entrust it to Brihaspati, Guru of the Devas, so that it may be installed in a suitable place and worshipped during Kaliyuga. Dwaraka was submerged in a deluge, but Brihaspati, with his prime disciple Vayu, the lord of wind, managed to retrieve the image. Whilst looking for a suitable place to install the deity, they met Parasurama, the avatar who was also going in search of the idol, to Dwaraka.

Parasurama led the Guru and Vayu to a lush green spot behind a beautiful lake. The yogi god Shiva and his consort Parvati who were spending time there in contemplation permitted Guru and Vayu to install and consecrate the idol there. From then on, the place came to be known as Guruvayur. Shiva and Parvati are said to have moved to the opposite bank and settled down at Mammiyur. The pilgrimage to Guruvayur is to this day considered incomplete without the worship at the Siva temple at Mammiyur.

That's as far as legends go. Historically, the earliest meeting of Guruvayur or rather Kuruvayur, comes from a Tamil work called *Kokkasandesam*. *Kurvai* means sea in Tamil and hence Kuruvayur. The earliest temple records date back to the 17ᵗʰ century. The temple is mentioned in the songs of the *Alwars*. By the end of the 16ᵗʰ century, Guruvayur was a popular pilgrimage centre in Kerala.

In 1760, the Dutch looted Guruvayoor and raided the treasures, the gold plate that covered the flagstaff and set fire to a part of the temple. In 1766, Hyder Ali captured Calicut and then Guruvayur. On the request of Srinivas Rao, the then governor of Malabar, Hyder Ali granted a free gift – *Devadaya*, and handed the temple back to the Hindus. In 1788, Tipu Sultan marched to Malabar. Fearing destruction, the priests hid the deity. Tipu Sultan destroyed the smaller shrines and set fire to the temple, but it was saved by a sudden and heavy down pour.

Later on, people like Chempakassery Namboodiri, Deshavarma Namboodiri and the Ullanad Pannikkars, offered everything from service to property. Worship at the temple was revived by the year 1900. In 1928, the Zamorin of Calicut was reinstated as the administrator of Guruvayur. In 1970, a massive fire broke out and the public, irrespective of caste creed or religion, rushed to join the fire fighting. There was massive destruction, but the sanctum sanctorum was saved. The temple was renovated and opened once again for worship on April 14, 1973.

Here, the names of two great and saintly persons who made Guruvayur famous have to be mentioned. *Melapathur Narayana Bhattathiri* (A.D. 1559-1632) was one and *Poonthanam* (A.D. 1547-1640) was the other.

Melapathur Narayana Bhattathiri, apart from being a scholar and mathematician, was the author of *Narayaneeyam*. The *Narayaneeyam* is a devotional Sanskrit work in the form of a poem or hymn, comprising 1036 verses and gives a summary of the great *Bhagavatha Purana*. The story goes that his guru Achyuta Pisharodi had painful arthritis. Unable to bear his guru's agony and suffering, Bhattathiri, by his yogic power, took the disease and relieved his guru. He soon discovered that the pain was excruciating and re- solved to make a pilgrimage to Guruvayur, confident that Guruvayurappan would relieve him of the disease.

While entering the temple, he is said to have met Thun- jath Ezhuthacchan, the author of Adhyatma Ramayana. Ezhuthacchan shocked him (an orthodox Brahmin) by say- ing *"Meen thottu Koottuka"* (start with the fish). On reflec- tion, Bhattatihiri realized that Ezhuthacchan was not asking him to eat fish but to start writing the Bhagavat, beginning with the story of Maha Vishnu's incarnation as the fish, the *Matsya Avatara*.

He then started with composing one *dasaka* (ten stanzas) a day, sitting before Sri Guruvayurappan and in a hundred days, had completed the *Narayaneeyam*. It is said that on the last day, he was blessed with a full vision of Guruvayurappan and got cured of his painful disease. Even today, *Narayaneeyam*, which is in Sanskrit, is held in great esteem in Kerala and read with great devotion.

Poonthanam, Melapathur's contemporary was not a great scholar but a true devotee of Sri Guruvayurappan. He is re- membered for his masterpiece *Jnanappana* which means 'the song of wisdom' and is written in Malayalam. Poonthanam was married at the age of twenty, but had no children for a long time. He is said to have prayed to Guruvayurappan, with tears in his eyes for a child and was finally blessed with a son. Poonthanam called for a grand celebration where everyone he knew was invited. Unfortunately and ironically, an hour before the ceremony the child died suddenly. Grief-stricken, Poonthanam renounced all worldliness and turned to Sri Guruvayurappan. His attitude underwent a sea change and he believed that the child god Krishna Guruvayurappan was his own child. He wrote, "Whilst little Krishna is dancing in our hearts, do we need little ones of our own?"

The Jnanappana begins and ends with:

Krishna Krishna, Mukunda Janardhana,
Krishna Govinda, Narayana Hare,
Achutananda Govinda Madhava
Satchitananda Narayana Hare.

"Here! Krishna Guruvayurappan, has come to take me to *Vaikuntam*, sing his praises," said Poonthanam, pointing upwards and letting go of his last breath, and passed away to be forever with his beloved Krishna.

✳ ✳ ✳ ✳ ✳

Let me now tell you about the wonderful *lila* Krishna enacted for me out of love and affection. In my autobiography, I have mentioned my friend Ananthanarayan and his father Vishwanath Iyer who worked for LIC of India. When Sri Vishwanath Iyer got transferred from Trivandrum to Thrissur, he invited me to Thrissur to see the annual festival of the great Vadakkunnathan Shiva Temple called *Thrissur Pooram*.

The *Thrissur Pooram* is celebrated on a grand scale with hundreds of richly decorated elephants lined up around the temple and the incessant beat of the *Chendai* drums, whilst the deities are taken in procession. It ends with fireworks on a colossal scale with all the buildings around the *pooram* grounds reverberating as if a thousand cannons have been fired together.

I eagerly accepted the invitation and enjoyed the festivities. Ananth could not come as he was studying for his engineering in Palaghat and was unable to get leave. The morning after the *pooram*, Vishwanatha Iyer woke me up early and said, "Come, we will go to Guruvayur. Hurry up, we have to wear a *mundu* and catch a bus." Guruvayur is not very far from Thrissur and it did not take us long. When we arrived, it was still dawn.

We took off our shirts and tied them around our waists, as men are required to enter the inner courtyard bare-bodied to the waist. At the entrance to the inner courtyard, I froze – a signboard said, 'Non-Hindus not allowed'. I said, "Uncle, I can't come in."

"Don't be silly," he said, "who is going to find out? In any case, I know you so well, you believe in Krishna. Also, you look like a Brahmin boy. Come!"

"No," I said, "I won't cheat. You go in and get me some *prasad*."

After trying to persuade me unsuccessfully, he went into the temple. I stood near the flag staff (*kodimaram*) and tried to view the sanctum sanctorum as best as I could. Everyone was chanting "*Narayana, Narayana, Guruvayurappa!*" My hair stood on end. Uncle Vishwanath Iyer came out with some sandalwood paste on his forehead, chanting "*Narayana, Narayana!*" He gave me some sandalwood paste and some flowers from the inner sanctum and said, "Let's go back."

I told him that I would stay back until evening and spend my time hanging around the premises which I loved so much.

"Ok," he said, "but be careful. Here, keep some money. You know where to catch the bus to Thrissur? Ok, come back before night fall."

I stayed on and after wandering around the outer courtyard for a while, I went to a nearby café and ate some *idlis* and *sambhar*. Hunger appeased, I walked to the side of the temple pond and sat down under the shade of a fairly old and gnarled tree. Suddenly, the tragedy of my situation hit me with full force and I started to weep loudly and uncontrollably, my whole body shaking.

A small crowd gathered. Someone asked, "Are you hungry? What's the matter?"

"Poor boy," said an old lady, and sitting down beside me stroked my head. Recovering after a while, I said I was fine and managed to dispense the group with my assurances that there was nothing to worry about. After that, I felt so tired that I lay down under the tree and fell asleep.

I had a wondrous dream. You may call it a dream but to me it was much more, for the great ocean of bliss that flowed through my heart that day is triggered every time, I chant or hear the words 'Narayana, Krishna, Krishna'. In my dream I was standing near the flag staff of the Guruvayur temple with folded hands, trying to catch a glimpse of the deity inside. I could barely see the outline which soon blurred, as tears had overwhelmed me.

All of a sudden, there came a loud, almost roaring sound of a conch being blown from inside the temple. My whole body trembled, and I said to myself, that must be the great *Panchajanya*, conch of Krishna, which was first heard during the fierce battle of *Kurukshetra* and made the mightiest of warriors tremble with fear. Then I saw something coming from inside the temple, almost hurtling towards the entrance. As it came nearer, I discovered that it was the sanctum sanctorum itself.

Inside stood the beautiful, dark complexioned, child god Krishna, with a divine smile on his face, beckoning me to come forward. I rushed towards the door. He stepped out of the sanctum and held me in a warm embrace. I was filled with great ecstasy. The sweet scent of tulsi and sandalwood surrounded me. Oh! How can I describe it? Loudly uttering "Krishna, Krishna," I woke up.

The ecstasy still pulsing through my body, I washed my face and feet in the pond and in a semi-conscious state ran into the inner courtyard. I stood near the sanctum sanctorum and watched the Namboodari priest worshipping my beloved Krishna, who smiled just as he had in my dream. I took the sandalwood paste, given to me as *prasad*, and walked out with faltering steps. In a matter of minutes, I was back to my stupid senses. Only a faint scent of sandalwood lingered.

I went around the temple along the path outside and then walked to the bus stand. In a short while, I was back in

Thrissur. When Vishwanath Iyer returned in the evening after work, I told him that I finally could not resist going inside the temple and had a great darshan. "I told you," was all he said, "You should have come in with me. Anyway you look very happy."

"Yes," I said, "very happy. Thank you, Uncle."

The special experience that I had, I kept a closely guarded secret and did not reveal even to him. I have treasured it in the depths of my heart and except for a few people to whom I have described bits and parts of the story, the whole episode has remained hidden to this day.

Now I open the floodgates of my heart for you, dear friends. Enjoy the sweet blessing of Krishna's love, as you read. As the *Srimad Bhagavatam* says, '*Satyam Param Dheemahi*' – I meditate upon the Truth, the Supreme.

6. A Journey to the Distant Past

As I write this chapter, I am aware of the reactions I am about to provoke. Good friends who love me inspite of my eccentricities and strange ways may finally conclude that I have gone mad and, in their kindness and concern, will try and persuade me to see a good psychiatrist. Some may dismiss it as bunkum and some as hallucinations, but I have to unburden myself of my memories. So whilst you read, if you do feel like reading at all, just remember that this is a wonderous world outside the confines of ordinary reasoning which only has the five senses to rely on.

* * * * *

My earliest, almost clear, memories of a past life go back thousands of years to the times of Sri Krishna, the Yadava hero and divine manifestation. My father, the *Rishi* Vishnupada and I, his only daughter Indumati, lived on the outskirts of the city of Indraprastha. We lived in a mud-walled, thatched *kutir* (cottage) in the forest that bordered the banks of the Yamuna, in the midst of beautiful flowering trees and creepers. Deer and peacocks wandered around freely.

My mother Renuka had died at childbirth and I was brought up by my father, with the help of the wives of other *Rishis* who lived in the forest. Being his only child, I was pampered by my father who loved me immensely. He treated me like a son and initiated me into the study of the Vedas, the chanting of the *Gayatri Mantra* and the practice of *Abhyasa* Yoga according to the *Yajnavalkya Sutras*. My father came from the same family as Dronacharya and though a Brahmin, had learnt archery and horse riding before he had retired into the forest to become a *Rishi*. He taught me both archery and riding and I learnt to ride on wild horses.

We led a peaceful and joyous life in Shrunga Vana, with the other *Rishis* and their families. As a *Rishiputri*, I led a chaste and disciplined life and by the time I was sixteen, was well accomplished in the study of the Vedas and *Vedaangas* including astronomy and related subjects. On the eve of my sixteenth birthday, my father, sitting under an ancient *Peepal* tree that stood nearby, said words that would change the course of my life. These were his words, "My child, the great divinity called Maha Vishnu has manifested himself in the form of a dark complexioned boy belonging to the Yadu clan, in the little town of Gokula, near the Brindavan grove. At the moment, he is running around and playing with the Gopas and Gopis (cowherds and cowgirls), but great events are scheduled to be set in motion by him. The great battle of Kurukshetra will be fought by the *Pandavas* and *Kauravas*. In the midst of which Krishna, as he is known, whilst acting as charioteer to Arjuna, one of the Pandava brothers, will teach him and give the world the simplified teaching of the Upanishads.

After Krishna's physical demise, the dark ages of Kali will begin where men will have short lives and except in rare cases, lose the capacity to penetrate the mysteries of nature or understand the Vedas. I feel my life will soon come to an end. Before that happens, I wish to travel to Brindavan with you. I might not reach there, but you will. There you will meet Krishna. After that, what happens, he knows and I don't. So, get ready to leave in the next two days. We will inform no one here. Keep the plan secret."

* * * * *

Two days later, one early morning, we started on our journey. It took several days. Sometimes, we found food and shelter in hermitages or in the houses of householders and sometimes we had to spend our time in the open, under the trees and eat whatever fruits and nuts we found. Twice, we were caught in heavy rains and chilly winds.

Three days short of Brindavan, my father took seriously ill. "Indu," he said to me, "I don't think I have the good fortune of seeing the physical manifestation of Narayana this time. You will see him. I am weak and will not recover from this illness. Help me go to the Yamuna. I shall let her take my body wherever she wishes. Proceed to Brindavan and look for a cowherd called Gunashila. He is my disciple. He and his wife Chandrika will look after you. It is time to go. Take me to the river."

With great difficulty I carried him to the river. With a lot of effort he let himself into the waters, shut off his breathing with *khechari*, chanted *Om* mentally with his sight fixed on the centre between the eyebrows and gave up his soul. His body was taken away by the river Yamuna.

I had lost everything now. My father, who was all that I had, was no more. Being a *Rishiputri*, I soon shed my grief and walked towards Brindavan. There, I enquired and located the house of Gunashila and Chandrika. They wept when they heard of the passing away of my father and adopted me as their own, for they were childless.

After many days, one evening, I told Chandrika, "My father said to me that the divine one has manifested himself as a young and handsome, dark-complexioned boy called Krishna in these parts. Have you seen him? Tell me about him. You think I can see him?"

Chandrika put her finger to her lips, "Shhh! Guna doesn't know but I am in love with him!" Her face was beaming with coyness and ecstasy. "Everyone knows him here. My husband thinks he is the divine Narayana but we the Gopikas know nothing about that. He is so lovely. He steals butter, plays pranks on us by taking away our clothes when we go for a bath in the river asking us to come out naked and take them from him. If he is divine, I think he is the incarnation of Kamadeva! O! My hair is standing on end."

I reprimanded her, "I think, from what you say, that you are talking about someone else. Can't be the one my father talked about, though the description of his complexion and features fit. Wait till I see him, if I can. He can't lure innocent, married women like this. I am a *Rishiputri* and no one can make me desire a man. I have full control over my senses. If I ever meet him, I am going to give him a few lessons on morality. Krishna or no Krishna, this is not done!"

"No wonder you Gopikas wear such heavy makeup and deck yourself with jasmine flowers. This fellow has your minds under his control through some black magic – *Krishnajaal*. I thought I was going to meet the great Lord but then my father can't be wrong."

Chandrika burst into peals of laughter. "You lovely child," she said, "wait till you hear the melody of his flute on a full moon night, wait my dear."

"We will see" I said, and proceeded for my daily meditation.

*****

Many days after this conversation, I confined myself to staying indoors, helping Chandrika with the household chores and concentrating on the study of ancient texts, some of which I had carried with me. I learnt to churn butter expertly, milk the cows and cook.

One late night, I was sitting alone in the inner courtyard which had no roof and ruminating on the stories about this Krishna I was hearing almost every day from the Gopis. I looked up and saw the full moon in all its naked glory, partly covered by a thin rainment of silvery white clouds. Then, I heard it. It came from a distance and slowly advanced towards me; the sweet melody of someone playing the flute. So beautiful was the music that I stood up and was rooted to the spot like a snake in front of a snake charmer. I caught myself swaying. A compelling desire to see the player and stand before him took hold of my heart. My hair stood on end and I was lost in ecstasy.

The trance was abruptly broken by the door of Guna's bedroom opening. Chandrika stood all decked up with jasmine flowers in her hair and black kohl in her eyes. Her silver anklets jingled as she ran out of the house. Her eyes had the glazed expression of a sleep walker and she hardly noticed me standing right in front of her. "Krishna," she muttered to herself and was gone.

I shook myself free from the temptation to follow her. After all I was a *Rishiputri*. Self-control was second nature. I looked into Guna's bedroom. He was fast asleep, as if drugged. I went back to my room and sat in *padmasana*. I meditated on my heart centre and wonder of wonders, the music came from my heart. A tiny bluish-black figure danced in the core of my consciousness. For a long time, I enjoyed it and then fell asleep.

Days passed and I still resisted. One evening at dusk, I walked up to the river to get some water. Whilst filling my water pot, I sensed someone standing behind me. I turned and saw him – a handsome, dark complexioned adolescent boy. His smile was the most beautiful one I have ever seen. He stroked my right shoulder and said, "Tonight is a full moon night. Come". Then he walked away.

I returned home and confided what had happened to Chandrika. "Ah!" she said, "I knew this would happen. Now come and get ready. Come."

Chandrika dressed me up, applied kohl to my eyes, painted my lips, decked me with jewellery, fixed jasmine flowers in my hair, applied sandal paste on my body and as soon as the moon came up above, led me to the grove. The music of the flute filled the air. I walked towards the source and came to the centre of the grove. Chandrika was left behind. I was alone, except for the full moon which was witness.

From behind an Ashoka tree, he suddenly appeared. He looked resplendent in yellow silk, a peacock feather stuck in his hair.

"Indu," he whispered, "come close to me. I am the one who dwells in your soul."

All my thoughts of being a distinguished, chaste daughter of a *Rishi* left me. The divine fragrance, the tenderness, the love, the security. O! Ecstasy that cannot be defined. I was lost in him. "Rishiputri," he teased me, "so now you are a *Gopi*. Come. Let's sit and talk. I need to tell you something. Wake up from your trance."

He led me to a rock sheltered by tall trees. "Sit down," he said and sat beside me. "The culmination of your austerities in many lives, has now brought you to me. You have now enjoyed my intimate embrace but much more needs to be done. You still have many unfulfilled desires."

"Go to Mathura to the hermitage of *Rishi* Dhyanasheela. He will accept you as a resident. Spend some years in austerities. When the great *Kurukshetra* war commences, disguise yourself as a soldier and fight on the side of the Pandavas. Your skill in archery and horse riding will be of great help. You will die in battle and I shall appear before you as your soul departs."

"After a long interval, you will be born in the family of my descendants as a warrior king in a desert kingdom. There, I shall send you a great *Siddha*, a manifestation of myself, who will become your Guru and guide you towards further spiritual evolution. Go now, my dear and remember I have embraced you and held you close to my heart." Having said that he vanished.

* * * * *

The next day, I bid farewell to Guna and Chandri and went to Mathura. The *Rishi* Dhyanasheela welcomed me to his hermitage. There I lived, studying the science of *Shakti chalan* or activating the *pranic* energies. When the *Kurukshetra* war broke out, I joined the forces of the Pandavas disguised as a man. I was an excellent archer, trained as I was by my father and many a strong Kaurava warrior fell to my powerful arrows.

Finally, an arrow from Ashwatthama's bow felled me. As I lay dying, Krishna came to me as promised, held my right hand with his left and laid his right hand on my forehead. I gave up my soul in peace looking at his loving eyes.

After several thousand years of earth time, after having reaped the benefits of my good karma in several realms, I was reborn as a Yadava chief in the deserts of Rajasthan amongst the shifting sand dunes and howling winds. The land had not yet acquired the name, it is now called Jaisalmer. That is another story and a very significant one, for my first contact with Sri Guru Babaji was established there. He was the great *Siddha* mentioned by Sri Krishna.

7. Swami Satchidananda: a Paragon of Humility and Self-effacement

I have met many a yogi, saint and sanyasin but never have I seen a soul so simple, humble and self-effacing as the late Swami Satchidananda of Anandashram, Kanhangad. Such fond memories, but before I speak of him, it's a good idea to say a few words about Anandashram and its founder Papa Ramdas and his devoted disciple, Mother Krishnabai. Swami Satchidananda was very close to Krishnabai.

Swami Ramdas was born in 1884 in Kerala and was given the name Vittal Rao. He came from a *Saraswat Brahmin* family from South Karnataka. His father initiated him into the mantra *Om Sri Ram, Jai Ram, Jai Jai Ram*. Around 1920, he gave up his wordly connections and wandered the length and breadth of India coming in contact with great spiritual masters like Sri Ramana Maharishi and Sri Aurobindo. After a profound and fascinating spiritual journey, he finally found his true spiritual source and remained absorbed in the bliss of self-realization.

In 1931, his devotees established the Anandashram (abode of peace) in Kanhangad, North Kerala, where he lived with Mother Krishnabai who had by his grace also attained spiritual fulfilment. Together, they worked tirelessly to improve the living conditions of the local people, founded a school, established a free medical clinic and set up a co-operative for weavers. They travelled extensively with the purpose of sharing the message of universal love and service. Above all, they were embodiments of love and compassion. The mantra *Om Sri Ram, Jai Ram, Jai Jai Ram* reverberates twenty four hours in Anandashram, spreading peace and radiating spiritual energy. Papa Ramdas passed away in 1963 and Mother Krishnabai took charge of the ashram. Mother Krishnabai attained *samadhi* in 1989.

Swami Satchidananda, who was known as Anantasivan before he took sanyas, came to Papa Ramdas at the age of thirty. In 1949, he left his family and came to the ashram for good. He was given sanyas and soon began his service to Papa Ramdas and Mother Krishnabai. After Mother's passing away, he inherited the mantle from his gurus and became the head of the ashram. On 12 October, 2008 he passed away peacefully, full of humility and love till his last day.

Although I had earlier studied the teachings of Swami Ramdas and Mother Krishnabai, I had not visited the ashram and with great regret I must say that I missed meeting both Papa and Mother. Much later, my dear friend Padukone Ramachandra Rao, a nephew of Papa Ramdas, took me to Anandashram for the first time. We drove down from Bangalore.

We reached the ashram by evening. My first impression was peace and tranquillity. There were quite a lot of people, it being a Sunday, but no one disturbed the quietness of the beautiful and unostentatious premises set on top of a hill amidst abundant greenery. We first visited the *samadhi* shrine of Papa Ramdas and Mother Krishnabai. A few people were meditating. After bowing down, Mr. Ramachandra

Rao took me to meet the administrator, who became a monk later adopting the name Swami Muktananda and now heads the ashram, since Swami Satchidananda's demise. He was clad in white. A very fine and kind gentleman, was my instant impression.

Soon, we were taken to Swami Satchidananda. We prostrated. Swami Satchidananda was already quite old and I had heard was not keeping well, but his face betrayed no sign of illness. He was tall, dark complexioned and wore the ochre robes of a renunciant. With a radiant smile, he talked softly and made enquiries about our well-being and how many days I intended to stay. "Make good use of the atmosphere here," he said in Malayalam.

"I have heard about you from P.R. Rao and I am sure you will enjoy the peace that Papa radiates here."

There were many people waiting to see him and so we paid our respects and took leave.

"Come again tomorrow," he said, "and please do attend the evening prayers at the shrine."

We were allotted simple rooms and I made a tour of the premises. Everything was simple but elegant. The dairy had a large number of cows. The *Akhanda Naama Japa* or the non-stop chanting of *Om Sri Ram, Jai Ram, Jai Jai Ram* was going on, with people taking turns to chant. In the evening, we filed into the shrine. Lovely *bhajans* were being sung and *aarati* performed. After a short meditation, I joined the queue of devotees to bow down before the pictures of Papa and the Mother and finally to Swami Satchidananda, who sat on one side, handing a flower to each person.

When my turn came, he handed me a red rose and whispered, "Everything all right?"

"Yes, Swamiji," I said.

The dining hall again served simple but tasty food. That evening, I enjoyed going into *samadhi* and most of the night I remained in a lovely trance. These were genuine souls and I wished Babaji had brought me here in my wandering days.

After two days, we bid farewell to Swamiji and left the ashram. After that I visited the ashram several times. Swamiji became very fond of me and I of him. On one of those visits, when I met Swamiji for a private interview, I requested him to initiate me into the mantra *Om Sri Ram, Jai Ram, Jai Jai Ram* which I already enjoyed chanting on my own. He looked into my eyes and asked softly, "You have decided finally to take it?"

"Yes," I said.

"Have you your Babaji's permission?"

"Yes," I said.

"Alright, come tomorrow morning and you will get the mantra."

I was thrilled beyond measure. The next day I went and met Swami Muktananda and he said that Swamiji had asked him to show me in.

I was ushered in. Swamiji said, "Ok, you will get the mantra but remember that it is Papa who arranges these things. I am nobody to initiate you. Papa Ramdas is the guru and he will initiate you."

I waited with bated breath. Perhaps, Swami Ramdas's spirit was going to whisper into my ear! What actually happened brought tears to my eyes, and taught me the supreme lesson of utter humility and surrender.

Swamiji produced a tape recorder and switched it on. "Hear carefully," he said, "this is the voice of Papa Ramdas. He is initiating you. He is your Guru and I am just a humble servant."

The voice of Papa Ramdas chanted in a gentle voice, "*Om Sri Ram, Jai Ram, Jai Jai Ram.*"

A thrill passed through my entire body and mind. I was bathed in the ecstasy of *Shuddha Brahma Paraatpara Ram.* O! How lucky to receive the mantra from Papa Ramdas himself and how blessed to sit at the feet of this great and gentle soul and receive his blessings. I prostrated and left without speaking much, for I had to get to my room, immersed as I was in the bliss of this great mantra. Two full hours, I stayed in that blissful realm. The next day, I returned to Bangalore carrying the grace in the secret chamber of my heart forever.

I visited the ashram several times after that and met many great souls and sadhaks. One of them, I met in the Anandashram for the first time, the ninety-one year old Swami Viswananda who had been with Ramana Maharishi and Papa Ramdas and who had the privilege of serving the saintly Ananda Moi Maa for well over twenty-five years. Also, my good friend and I would say a truly sincere *sadhak*, Sri Ajay Kumar Singh.

On one of my visits, I also met three unknown sadhus, whom I consider to be fairly advanced spiritually.

A dear friend, a sincere and learned seeker and one whom I consider my elder brother, Srikanth, who publishes beautiful books on spiritual subjects, lives close by and I never miss an opportunity to pay my respects to him.

The last time I visited the ashram was when Swamiji was very ill and hospitalised in Hyderabad. He had sent word through Swami Muktananda that I should be invited to hold a *satsang* along with Swami Shankarananda of the Rama-krishna Mission during *Guru Poornima* at the ashram.

Since Swamiji was very ill, he was not expected to attend. But to everyone's surprise he arrived that morning, although he was too ill to attend the satsang. Before returning, the next day, I bid farewell to him. When I stood up after pros-trating, I felt this was the last time I would see him. His kind eyes seemed to say, 'I am tired of this body and want to shake it off. We will meet in total 'Freedom'.'

8. Moving in Space

Here I sit, in the Himalayan foothills. As I see the Ganga flow past, from the balcony of my room, old memories return – a young disciple sitting beside Babaji, in the Arundhati cave, looking at the river that has flown for centuries.

I say to Babaji, "From childhood I have had dreams in which I fly through the air, sometimes so fast that seeing electric lines and low branches of trees I actually duck low to avoid them. Sometimes I saw strange places which I haven't seen before. I think I have seen the Himalayan ranges several times in these dreams. When I wake up, the details are forgotten. Are these more than dreams born out of the latent desires in my sub-conscious mind or is there something more to it?"

Babaji said, "Son, most of our dreams are a garbled mixture of the thoughts in our sub-conscious mind and the actual experiences of one's subtle body called the 'Linga Sharira' or 'Sukshma Sharira', which in all human beings leaves the physical body, the 'Sthula Sharira', when the physical body is in deep sleep. The brain has an in-built mechanism to wipe out the details of this night-time journey, so that all you remember when you wake up is a jumble of faint memories from the travels undertaken by one's subtle body and the contents of the sub-conscious; except in certain rare cases of '*Yoga Bhrastas*', those who have been yogis in their previous births and are reborn to complete their unfinished journey."

Babaji's eyes twinkled as he said, "There are techniques, however, to leave your physical body and travel in your subtle body consciously and remember all the details."

I said, "I would love to learn this because I remember feeling like a free bird soaring in the air when I was in the dream state, but it's all in your hands. I shall do it only if you think it is right for me and it will not distract me from the main goal."

Babaji said, "Perhaps, you should start practising. I shall put all precautions in place for your safety and see that you are not distracted from the main goal – call it *moksha*, *kaivalya* or *nirvana*. This will enable you to visit and keep in touch with me, when I am away physically, especially in areas not accessible easily by ordinary means."

Babaji then went into a description of the characteristics of the subtle body, before instructing me in some of the techniques of projecting the subtle body out of my physical frame.

* * * * *

The *linga sharira* or the subtle body is made up of fine matter invisible to the ordinary eyes and is shaped like the physical body and fits exactly onto the physical body. It is also called *kaama roopa*, because the inner self or atman manifests its innate joy through the subtle body when the physical body fulfils its desires through the sense organs.

Although the subtle body is almost a duplicate in form of the physical body, when it stands by itself detached from the physical, it appears younger and more beautiful to the eyes of the clairvoyant. It cannot be seen by ordinary eyes and is fully formed when a child reaches the age of eight.

"Clairvoyance," Babaji said, "is not so common and is possessed only by highly advanced yogis." He warned me especially against those who pretend to be clairvoyant, but are only people with a heightened sense of imagination that has gone haywire or mere pretenders, taking advantage of weak and gullible minds.

For the yogi who has overcome his desires, the subtle body fades away and disintegrates when the physical body dies and the atman is henceforth clothed in a pure vehicle called the 'causal body' or the *karana sharira*. For others, the subtle body called the *linga sharira* carries, to use the words of Krishna in the *Bhagavad Gita*, 'all its *vasanas* or desires in seed form, like the wind carries the perfume of the flowers', till it occupies a new body to indulge and enjoy the latent desires.

Apart from being the same shape as the physical body and not being visible, except to those with extra sensory perception, the subtle body can see, hear and smell but does not have the capacity to touch. If one is in the subtle body and tries to grasp an object in the physical world, the fingers would simply go through the object and therefore, it is not possible to carry back any object that is seen. Being made up of subtle matter, the subtle body can pass through walls and penetrate physical barriers.

In the beginning, it is not possible to move far from the physical body, but by and by, one learns to travel long distances in the subtle body and come back at will. The connection between the subtle body and the physical body, for most people, is at the navel centre, except for the yogi who deliberately ejects the subtle body through the centre between his eye-brows, the *ajna chakra*. This enables the yogi, after long years of practice, to travel not only in the physical world but also to other spheres and realms. There are other extra-terrestrial bodies outside Earth in the space called *akasha* or the Milky Way. Only the most developed yogis can travel through all these levels.

* * * * *

At one of the sessions, I interrupted Babaji and asked, "Are ghosts, which people report they have seen or felt, the *linga sharira* or the subtle bodies of travelling yogis or the subtle bodies of those whose physical bodies have died?"

Babaji said, "Only in rare and special circumstances this is possible, because the subtle bodies of people whose physical bodies have died cannot remain for very long in this world. Great yogis, however, who have a special function to perform, might retain their causal bodies or *karana sharira*. They may be visible, only to those who have developed special vision. Even those who have not developed special powers of perception may at times see non-physical entities when the limbic system in their brain is excited by emotions like great fear, religious ecstasy, grief or the use of mind-altering drugs."

"Generally, sightings reported as ghosts are what may be called 'etheric doubles'. Consider the case of a healthy hu-

54

man being having lost his life suddenly through an accident or suicide. Every human body contains chemicals in its cells which through reactions produce an electric charge, which assumes the shape of the body from which it originates. In the case of sudden deaths, the body may be cremated or buried or destroyed but the electric charge that had assumed the shape of the body is thrown out and remains independent for a while till the charge subsides and finally disappears."

"Since this etheric double, as one might call it, is connected sympathetically to the places and objects associated with the physical body which was responsible for its origin, till the charge is completely dissipated it hovers around those familiar places and objects to which it is magnetically attracted to these."

Babaji said, "The *sukshma sharira* or the subtle body has ascended to the higher realms where it can rest and then decide, with the help of guides, its future course of rebirth based on future evolutionary factors."

"Remember, however, that the etheric double which is mistaken for a ghost and appears under special circumstances, including a foggy night apart from what we discussed, has no intelligence or will of its own and is merely an electric charge that causes no harm to anyone except that sudden sighting may make a weak heart stop beating."

"Deviant yogis who dabble in the black arts sometimes use the etheric double, directing it with their will power, to appear in certain places and behave in a certain manner to sow the seeds of fear in the hearts of those whom they wish to harm. This is partly what is called black magic and they have ways and means of keeping the etheric double from disintegrating, which it would have otherwise done in the natural course of things."

"Those who chant spiritually charged mantras like *Om Namah Shivayah* or *Om Namo Narayana* or Quranic verses specifically meant for such purposes, can negate the energies of an etheric double and cause it to disintegrate instantly."

"Yogis who are highly advanced have nothing to fear from the etheric double and so also others who are protected by their advanced spiritual teachers. The devout who surrender to the Divine are naturally protected from such evil intentions of the practitioners of the black arts."

"However, most of those who claim to be black magicians are merely frauds, working on the fears and gullible nature of the general public. The rare ones, who really practise black magic, usually end up being victims of their own evil thoughts and usually die miserable deaths."

* * * * *

One clear night when I had developed for a short while, the capacity to see beyond my ordinary senses by practising the special exercises taught by Babaji, I stood outside my *kutir* at midnight and could see silver-blue strands emerge from the roofs of the small number of *kutirs* around, with the faint outline of the subtle bodies of the sadhus who lived inside attached to these cords. I remembered what Babaji had said about all human beings leaving their physical bodies and being in their subtle bodies, whilst the physical body slept.

In the next chapter, we will discuss those pieces of information that may be revealed at this moment about the different techniques taught by Babaji to consciously project this subtle body from the physical. As Babaji said, "The main thing that prevents one from coming out from the physical body is the belief that it cannot be done. This is an in-built response so that people in general, remain without the capacity to shake free from the gross body and fly freely like a bird!"

9. Simple Techniques for Out-of-Body Travel

I shall now discuss the actual techniques of projecting the subtle body (astral body) as promised in the previous chapter.

Many methods were taught by Babaji but I have permission to reveal only two. I am also prohibited from discussing a specific breathing technique that eases astral projection. But that need not act as a dampener. Using one of the two simple techniques, it is possible to project out of the physical body. The main obstacle to astral projections is the belief that it is not possible to do so or that there is no such thing as astral projections. The moment you believe that most human beings can and that it is fairly simple and straight forward to astral project, you have opened the door to actually moving out of your physical body and floating around.

So here is technique 1:

This is the simplest and, although it may take a little time to succeed, the safest.

When you lie down to sleep at night, switch off all the lights (lights distract). If you feel sleepy, remove the pillow, otherwise you may end up sleeping instead of projecting. Wear loose and comfortable clothes and adopt the *shavasana* posture but with feet together, not spread out.

Breathe deeply and calmly. Now visualise a place where you would like to go or think of your best friend or favourite person who you would like to visit. With eyes closed, actually feel that you are passing through the bedroom door and walking out through the gate as you would normally do. Walk along the path that leads to your friend's house or sit on your cycle and cycle away. To start with, visualise only places close by, walking distances, like your favourite park.

Once you reach the place in your imagination, sit quietly on a bench or lie down on the grass and see everything in detail. Don't get excited if a big dog comes near you, because the dog cannot see you. One day, you will actually be there in your subtle body and see and hear everything. To go back to the physical body, you only need to think of going back or stretch out on the lawn and sleep. When you wake up, you will be in the physical body. There is no need to fear about what would happen if you cannot come back, because you actually cannot stay away for long. You might be brought back with a jerk and may wake up with a bad headache.

Please remember that you can feel, hear and smell everything in your astral body but cannot feel with your hands, taste or take back anything, as your hands will pass through all objects. Also, although you can see others, others cannot see you unless they have special vision, like great yogis or clairvoyants. Your astral body can go through solid walls and enter anywhere.

The first time you are out of your body, it is such a beautiful experience, floating around like a cloud, that you will feel terrible when you get back to the physical body. It is as if you have entered a heavy shell which you have to carry around. It takes time to get accustomed to both feelings.

The most important thing is to note down immediately all your experiences in the astral body as soon as you are back. The brain is likely to forget the experiences, so write when your memory is still fresh. If you fall asleep during the projection, you will remember, vaguely, when you wake up. Write it down immediately. In an hour or so, the memory will be lost.

Bon Voyage my friend!

* * * * *

Now the second technique, which is a little more difficult but when learnt is a sure shot method. The yogis use this or a similar but more advanced technique. So here we go:

Wear loose and comfortable clothing and if you are practising during the day, make sure that all the curtains are drawn and there is no light to distract you. Dim light that filters through the curtains is okay.

If you are trying it out at night, all lights should be switched off. Never practise after a heavy meal as you are more likely to sleep. If you have had a full meal, leave an interval of at least two hours before you practise.

Lie in the *shavasana* posture with feet together on a comfortable bed. Use no pillow. You may roll up a towel and support your head so that your head stays in a relaxed position facing the ceiling. Soft and slow music is permissible but if you can do without it, it is better.

Now, with open eyes stare at the dim outline of the ceiling. Then close your eyes and actually feel that you are floating near the ceiling, facing the ceiling. Visualise your body in great detail. Then visualise the seven centres of energy called the chakras as whirling lights, starting with the base chakra at the bottom of the spine to the last chakra on the top of the head. Picture all of them together like electric blue whirling circles.

Relax, do not become tense. First, do the visualisation as if you are painting a picture in complete tranquillity. Don't think that you are trying to come out of the body, think instead that you have already come out and are hovering near the ceiling with your chakras softly whirling. Stay with that. After a while, maybe on the first day itself or later, you will feel a floating sensation or a lifting sensation as if you are going up on a lift. A gentle sway, and you realise that you are floating up there. Turn around and you will see the physical body lying there on the bed.

It will take a few seconds to realise that it is your body because to see oneself face to face is different from seeing a mirror image.

You are now ready for astral travel. In the beginning, go only to nearby places. As you get more experience, you can move further away. In fact, if you can visualise the person or place you want to visit clearly, you will be there at the speed of thought.

So enjoy your new found freedom and fly around. Remember, you need have no fear of not being able to return.

You cannot remain outside for long even if you want to. It is nature's law that you have to return. Only at death the connecting silver cord is severed, so that you are free of the heavy physical cage forever.

10. Travelling Free: My Out of Body Experiences

I write this sitting in my little cabin at Breitenbush Hot Springs, in the State of Oregon, United States of America. Breitenbush is a beautiful retreat centre built on an old Native Indian sacred place. Outside my window stand tall and majestic trees. I can hear the river flow by, not far away. This is my eighth visit to Breitenbush, where I teach meditation to small groups, mostly Americans, every year.

At night, I love drifting about in my subtle body. The sacred chants of the native Indians are still carried by the wind, if you have the ears to hear. More of all that later. Now, about my first real out-of-body experience. If you are a Richard Dawkins, Martin Gardner or James Randi fan, please suspend your judgements for a while. We are entering largely unexplored realms beyond the rational framework of the conditioned mind that loves to disbelieve.

* * * * *

I was living in a *kutir* (a small cottage) on the banks of the Ganga, a little beyond Laxman Jhula, when I had my first out-of-body experience. Babaji had said he was off to Mukteshwar, in the Almora district for a few months, for reasons best known to him. I had been practising a certain technique

63

taught by Babaji, for projecting my subtle body, for more than six months without much success. That particular night I was lying down on my bed, preparing to sleep, when it happened spontaneously without me practising the technique. As sleep almost took over, I remember that the last thought on my mind was, "Where could Babaji be?"

A slight swaying motion and a gentle tug and I found myself floating free and weightless, looking down on this body called 'M'. It took me a few seconds to realise that what I was looking down at was actually my body, as this was the first time I was looking at myself from outside. I looked a little different from the image in the mirror that I was accustomed to.

When I discovered that I was indeed in my subtle body, I decided that the best thing to do under the circumstances was to try and look for Babaji. Was he in the Arundhati cave or Mouni Baba's or in his favourite hideout in Cheerbasa on the way to Gaumukh?

As my desire to see Babaji became stronger, I felt myself speeding headlong towards an unknown destination. Forgetting that I was not in my material body I ducked a few times under high-tension electric lines. Snow covered peaks made their appearance. I was flying over the Himalayas but the terrain looked unfamiliar. I certainly was not in Uttarakhand. Then I saw the sand dunes and the great lake and realised that this was probably Mansarovar in Tibet. It was confirmed, when I saw Mount Kailash, looking exactly as it did in the many pictures I had seen.

On one side of Mount Kailash was a deep gorge where I landed smoothly. It was the annual pilgrimage season and

I saw pilgrims performing the circumambulation – some on foot, others on horses. Yaks, loaded heavily with luggage, walked beside them. I knew I was invisible.

In the gorge where I landed, there was no one to be seen. I was wondering where Babaji was, when I noticed a fairly large crevice in the rock to my left. As I tried to peer into it, I found myself slipping through it and entering the mouth of a cave. The cave stretched deep into the cliff and was lit by a dim violet glow from some unknown source. I kept going in until I came to a circular chamber where the cave ended. My astral heart skipped a beat. Seated in front of a *dhuni* (sacred fireplace) was Babaji. Facing him, and on the other side of the fire, was an old Tibetan monk in russet and yellow robes.

As soon as I set my eyes on Babaji, I prostrated full length on the floor. When I sat up, Babaji chuckled and said, "I can see you but remember no one else can. You are not in your physical body."

"Oh!" I said, "I forgot. Shall I prostrate to the venerable monk? Can he see me?"

"No" Babaji said, "he can't, but you should prostrate."

I looked at the monk. For a moment, a puzzled expression appeared on his face. He was probably wondering what was going on, for he could not have heard my voice. It was as if Babaji was talking into thin air. Babaji then explained to him and he nodded. I guessed he was a great and learned man, although he was not clairvoyant.

"Sit down," said Babaji. "This, your first successful out-of-body trip was entirely due to your effort. Good! But coming here and seeing me would not have been possible if I did not want it to happen. As a matter of fact, I willed you to come here for an important purpose and therefore opened the barrier I normally use to shield myself from astral travellers."

"Now, let's get down to business. This Lama is the caretaker for a series of caves not far from here, where relics, left by extra-terrestrial visitors who came to earth many thousands of years ago, are preserved. They came from a planet in a constellation many light years away."

"They were deputed by still further advanced extra-terrestrial beings to teach earthlings certain yogic and scientific secrets including the primary principles of language. They landed on the summit of the Kailash peak and then moved towards the caves where you will presently go. The Bonpos of pre-Buddhist Tibet have a belief that their founder descended from heaven on to Mount Kailash. This mythology of theirs is based on the arrival of these advanced extra-terrestrials."

"Seven of them, the *Sapta Rishis*, landed here. After teaching a selected few the knowledge that had to be imparted, the *Sapta Rishis* prepared to return but their space craft developed a snag. They had to stay for a while, until help came from their realm."

"Two of the advanced extra-terrestrials died, because they could not adjust to the new environment. Eventually, the mechanics who arrived set the aerial vehicle right and they departed leaving behind their dead. The dead *Sapta Rishis* were now perfectly mummified to be viewed by special individuals from future generations."

"You will see all that when I take you there. I have taken permission from the venerable Lama. Prostrate to him and let us go."

Babaji then lay down on his folded blanket and in no time his subtle body was beside me. His physical body was left under the Lama's care.

We travelled together passing through ruins of a city and reached a series of caves hidden well by cliffs and ruins. We entered a tunnel that looked like bomb shelters built by the Japanese in the Andaman Islands during World War II.

Soon we reached a large circular cave with small passages leading to smaller caves. It was lit by a beautiful cool violet light that came from a cavity on the roof. A number of strange devices were placed in glass containers all along the walls of the cave.

"The violet light," said Babaji, "is powered by nuclear energy and left here by the visitors from outer space. The technology used is yet undiscovered by our scientists. It is supposed to be lit for another one hundred years, after which the intensity may reduce."

Babaji pointed out to the various microscope and telescope like devices in the glass cases and explained about them. They were all precision instruments brought by the extra-terrestrials for various purposes. In a small vacuum container were little white cubes.

"These," explained Babaji, "are nuggets made of a special material that are packed with super-nutritional substances. The great beings brought them along. A small bit of it diluted in a glass of water, is enough to sustain their bodies for a hundred years or more. Unfortunately, the cells of human bodies are not capable of absorbing such high doses of nutrition and will in fact begin to multiply, if ingested, faster than the fastest cancerous cells known to humankind and lead to disaster."

In a fairly big container were flat discs made of a white shiny material. Something like Egyptian hieroglyphs were engraved on them. Babaji explained that these were codes which, when decoded with the help of special devices not yet perfected by mankind, will reveal information about outer space realms and civilizations and the story of many previous visits by extra-terrestrials. They would also describe those rare instances, when specially developed humans were taken to these far space realms and brought back after awakening special centres in their brains, which distinguished them from ordinary human beings in many ways.

In another circular container, were two large flat discs, which Babaji indicated were the two super magnets from the aerial vehicle of the extra-terrestrials. It was because these discs had malfunctioned that they had to remain for a long time on earth waiting for replacements from their home planet. Babaji said that the magnets were so powerful, even now, that they were kept in a special insulated container.

Finally, he took me into one of the passages that led to an enclosure. Inside were two glass coffins that contained perfectly mummified bodies of the two beings that had expired due to being unable to withstand the changed environment on earth. They were almost ten feet in height, were fair in complexion, almost milk white and had beautiful features. One could not say if they were male or female. Their faces and bodies were absolutely hairless and wrinkle free. They had thick, brown shoulder length hair and wore ornaments that seemed to be made of gold and diamonds.

Babaji said, "These great beings were androgynous. The *Ardhanareeswara* concept, where Shiva is depicted as half-male and half-female, comes from this. They possessed the reproductive organs of both sexes in one body."

"Whatever can be revealed to you at this point has been done," said Babaji. "No more now. It is time to go. You can go back to your *kutir*. I will see you after a month." I prostrated to Babaji and journeyed back to my *kutir* at Laxman Jhula.

* * * * *

Over the years, after that first experience of mine, I have travelled to many locations on this earth as well as outside, seeing wonders that would not be believed if stated, including the fact that there are worlds entirely peopled (or is it *snaked*) by hooded serpents and other strange creatures, not to mention the higher worlds where celestial beings live.

In the prevailing atmosphere of scepticism and cynicism that seems to have enveloped most of human thinking, the less said the better. Let's move on to other things.

11. Meeting Sri Guru Babaji: the Jaisalmer Connection

This is the story of my birth in the deserts of Rajasthan in the area close to Jaisalmer, even before the Jaisalmer fort was built and Jaisalmer got its name. As Lord Krishna had said in Brindavan, I was born in a *Bhati* Rajput clan that claimed descent from Sri Krishna's Yaduvansh and therefore belonged to the Lunar dynasty. It was also a very important turning point of my life for, as promised by Sri Krishna, no other than the great Siddha Sri Guru Babaji would come into my life. This was my first contact with Sri Guru.

* * * * *

Let me start at the beginning. The erstwhile rulers of the desert kingdom which lies in the Thar Desert are *Bhati* Rajputs claiming descent from Sri Krishna. In the ninth century I was born as Rawal Deoraj, a great warrior of the *Bhati* clan. Being a great archer, horse rider and fearless warrior, I went to war with many neighbouring tribes and expanded my kingdom. All was going well. I was acknowledged as the greatest warrior of the desert. Even the Pathan chiefs across the border feared Deoraj.

Then, I fell in love with the beautiful daughter of a neighbouring chieftain named Karan. Her name was Karni. Her father had invited me to his tent to negotiate a joint war against a rival chief. She came in to serve food and that was the first time I saw her. I fell in love. A few days later, I took the risk of riding to her father's territory in the dead of the night. Tip toeing to her tent, I woke her up. It was a moonlit night. She came out without fear and we stood looking at each other. Not wanting to lose time, I laid bare my heart. She giggled and ran back into her tent saying, "talk to my father. I too loved you the moment I saw you. Now go away before my father's guards see you."

At the next meeting I had with Chief Karan, I expressed my love for his daughter. Chief Karan was not opposed to our marriage but wanted my family to negotiate the proposal. Since my family had no objection, the families met and the marriage was fixed. There was one problem which we did not think was serious. Chief Karan had previously agreed to give his daughter in marriage to a neighbouring chieftain, but Karni had refused to marry him. This was conveyed to the chieftain's family by her father and that is where the matter stood.

On the day of the marriage, as we exchanged garlands of rare desert flowers, the wedding party was ambushed. Nearly nine hundred guests attending the wedding, mostly unarmed, were massacred. My father, my bride Karni, Chief Karan and many relatives on both sides lay dead. I escaped. Running out of the tent into the desert, pursued by soldiers of the rival chieftain, tired and exhausted, I finally reached a small oasis called the *Jogisaar*. It was reputed that a great yogi had his residence there.

From a thatched cottage, a yogi emerged. He bore all the marks of a Brahmin holy man. The vertical marks on his forehead, the sandal wood symbols drawn all over his body, the copper earrings, the *tulsi* beads on his neck, the tuft on his head and above all, the sacred thread. He greeted me. I touched his feet. "Come in quickly," he said "your pursuers will be here soon. Go into the kutir and shave off your hair, beard and moustache. Leave only a tuft on your head. I have left a razor, water, polished mirror and a cloth. Wear the caste marks, the sacred threads and beads and the loin cloth you will find. Then sit in the courtyard with me. We shall eat our midday meal from the same copper plate."

I hurried in, got ready and soon we were sitting together eating from the same plate in the outer courtyard. Four henchmen of the murdered chieftain Akhai soon arrived. They got down from their horses and saluted the holy man. "Sorry to interrupt your meal Sir," they said, "we are looking for the coward Deoraj, who likes to call himself *Rawal*. Did you see a warrior pass by or did he ask for water or food?"

"As far as I know," said the holy man, "neither my disciple nor I have seen any traveller for the last two days. If you wish to have water, please help yourself to the water pot outside. I would appreciate, if you would leave us in peace. Clanging of swords and neighing of horses disturb our spiritual practices. If we see anyone, we will send information to your chief. When you see him, give him our blessings. *Namo Narayana.*"

After drinking some water, they bowed down and thanked the holy man and galloped away.

After they left, he turned to me, "Eat and rest for a while. That we were eating from the same plate made them believe

72

that you were a Brahmin disciple. Also, I had to work a little magic. I am the *Siddha*, who Sri Krishna promised to send to you in a previous birth when you were the daughter of a Brahmin *rishi*. You don't remember, of course. I am the one called Sri Guru. Many spiritual seekers simply call me Babaji. I will remain for a complete *yuga* to guide and hasten the evolution of spiritual seekers. Later, I shall tell you more. Now take rest."

Tired and exhausted as I was, I fell asleep almost instantaneously in the cottage. When I woke up it was evening. The sun was setting. I came out and saw the great Sri Guru gazing at the setting sun and chanting something. I quietly sat beside him.

I spent a week with him and was initiated into certain yogic practices. Babaji also revived a small part of the memory from my past life when I was Indumathi, the daughter of the Rishi Visnupada. Babaji taught me the basic principles of leadership.

Before I left him, Babaji blessed me and made a few predictions. Two centuries later, he said, Jaisal the eldest son of the then Maharawal of Lodarva, also Deoraj by name, will be passed over at the death of his father and the kingdom would be usurped by a younger half-brother of his. Jaisal would then take the help of an Afghani Muslim invader, Shihabuddin of Ghor and will recapture Lodarva, after sacking the city for many days. When he reclaims his throne, Lodarva would be a ruined city.

Whilst searching for a new place to set up his capital, Maharawal Jaisal will find a massive rock formation, jutting out of the surrounding sands. There Jaisal would meet

Babaji's close disciple Maheshwarnath who would then be living under the name of Eesulnath.

Eesul would reveal the story that ages ago, Sri Krishna and Bhima visited the hill and that the spring that sprang up there in the middle of the desert was created by Sri Krishna to quench Bhima's thirst. Encouraged by Eesulnath's story that Krishna had himself predicted the establishment of a kingdom on that spot by a descendant of his own Yadu clan, Jaisal would establish his new capital on the hill by building a mud fort and naming it Jaisalmer after himself.

Babaji said I had much to travel on the path of spiritual evolution. After being born many years later, as a Muslim queen in the south of India, I would then meet the great being Sadashiva Brahmendra of Nerur and be initiated by him. In the birth after that, I would be purified enough to be Sri Guru's personal disciple and would be born in an orthodox Brahmin family which would migrate from Benaras to the Himalayas, near Badrinath.

Due to a certain turn of events, which would help in further expanding my consciousness and the learning of new lessons, I would again be born in Bengal and then in a Muslim family in the south, this time as a male. Then Maheshwarnath, his disciple, would be deputed to find me while still very young. It would be in this life, when people would know me as 'M', that I would reveal all the connections.

At the end of my training, I prostrated at Babaji's feet and left. Working from my hideout in an abandoned monastery of the *Nath Sampradaya*, I soon gathered my men and formed a formidable army. Clan after clan was defeated and their territories were annexed and for a while, I made Derawar my capital. Later, I captured Lodarva from a powerful Rajput chief and made it my capital. Lodarva remained the capital of the Rawals for quite some time.

Death came at a ripe old age. I was perfectly healthy at that time. The yogic practices that I had been taught stood me in good stead. One day, I fell down whilst riding my horse and broke my neck. I succumbed to the injury and surrendered to Sri Guru Babaji at the time of my death.

12. The Unknown Yogi

Sitting on the steps of Munshi Ghat in Benaras one evening, and watching the boats go by on the river Ganga, I remembered one of my previous visits to the ancient city. That was when I was working in Delhi as the joint editor of *Manthan*, published by Nanaji Deshmukh. I had planned to resign and join *New Wave*, a tabloid edited by Ganesh Shukla, an ex-journalist from the Leftist newspaper 'Patriot'. I took a week's leave and travelled to Benaras before I quit.

This was the time, when Maheshwarnath Babaji had banished me from his presence for two years, saying that I needed to live independently and stand on my own feet. I was secretly hoping that I would run across Babaji somewhere in the ghats or in the narrow streets that lead to Kashi Vishwanath. Unfortunately, I did not.

One evening, sitting in a dilapidated *mantap* above the Manikarnika Ghat and looking down at the burning corpses, I turned to the right and came upon a shaven-head sanyasin carrying a wooden staff, who I guessed belonged to the *Dasanami* order of monks, sitting in contemplation. I was a little surprised because the monks belonging to the order founded by Adi Sankaracharya usually do not frequent places near the burning ghats.

After half an hour or so, he opened his eyes and looked toward me. I summoned up the courage to walk up to him, greeted him and prostrated with folded hands. '*Namo Narayana*,' he said, a typical greeting of the Dasanami order.

"May I sit down?" I asked.

"Sit down," he said.

Then he enquired what I was doing there, who I was and where I came from. I gave him some of the details and added that a great yogi by name Maheshwarnath Babaji, who belonged to the *Nath sampradaya*, was my guru and that I had lived with him in the Himalayas for some years.

"Ah, so you're a *Nath*," he said. "But you're not a *kaan-phata*" (a term used to indicate the ear rings worn by the people belonging to the *Nath* lineage, by puncturing the car-tilage in their ears).

"Babaji exempted me from that practice," I said.

"Umph" he said, "you know that we, *Dasanamis* in gene-ral, do not take kindly to the *Nath sampradaya*; though personally I am of the opinion that there are valuable inputs that the *Nath* teachings provide for those engaged in spiritual practices."

I asked him, "Do you know of any great yogis in this area?"

He said, "There are a few unknown yogis, I am sure. The great *Vedantin* Karpatriji resides in Benaras and I would have recommended that you pay a visit to him. Unfortu-nately, at the moment he is in Badrinath."

He paused for a moment and then said, "There is a yogi who lives in a small *kutir* all by himself, close to the Assi Ghats. I have heard that at one time he was a *dandi swami*, belonging to the *Dasanami* order, who abandoned his *dandi* in the Ganga and now does not belong to any order. Since you are so keen to meet a great yogi and seem to be sincere in your pursuit of the spiritual path, it may be a good idea to go and see him. I am told that he rarely speaks, but who knows, may be you will have some luck." With that he stood up, said, "*Namo Narayana*" and walked away.

It was too late to go to Assi Ghat, so I spent some more time at Manikarnika and walked back to my shabby little room at Peshwa Ghat. The caretaker of the neglected old building had given me the room for a rent of Rs. 50 per night. I drank a hot cup of milk provided by him, put the cash which I had in my pocket into the rucksack and fell asleep on the *charpoy*. I slept deeply.

The next morning, I woke up pretty early. I could hear the gongs and bells of the morning *aarti*. I walked down the steps of the ghat, took a dip in the Ganga, came back to my room, picked up my rucksack and started walking towards the Assi Ghat. The pink glow of the sun about to rise suffused the atmosphere with a calmness and tranquility which was peculiar to Benaras. Some boats had already started plying. By the time I reached the Assi Ghat, the sun had half risen and looked like a golden disc shining in the horizon. I was reminded of the verse from the *Ishavasya Upanishad*:

> *Hiranmayena paatrena*
> *Satyasyaa pihitam mukham*
> *Tattvam pushan apaavrunu*
> *Satyadharmaaya drishtaye*

O Sun, the Controller! Remove the dazzling golden disc from your face so that I, the righteous seeker looking for the Truth, may see you face to face.

At Assi Ghat I made some enquiries and soon located the yogi. He lived in a *kutir* close to the ghats, with a small verandah in front. I walked up to the *kutir*. He was sitting on the verandah. He was a thin, short man, sunburnt, almost brown with a flowing grey beard and thick hair neatly tied up into a bun on the crown of his head.

He was wearing only a *kaupin* and sitting in *padmasana*, looking calmly at the flowing waters of the Ganga. The most distinguishing features I noticed were his large and tranquil eyes. Around his neck he wore *rudraksh* beads. I noticed that he did not wear any of the paraphernalia of the *Nath* sect and did not have a *dhuni*. I prostrated, stood up and said, "I was told that you were in *mauna* (silence). I don't wish to disturb you. I would just like to meditate in your presence".

He smiled kindly and surprised me by saying, "It's alright. I don't stick to rules fanatically. I see your sincerity. Come here and sit on the verandah."

So I climbed up on the verandah and sat beside him on a folded blanket which was already there. "See," he said, "I was expecting someone to come today." Then he made enquiries about me. I gave him a brief account of my life to which he listened patiently. I saw him perk up when I mentioned Maheswarnath Babaji. "Oh," he said, "so you are a disciple of Maheshwarnath Babaji. I had heard that he rarely takes disciples. You would be happy to know that though we haven't met each other; he is my *gurubhai*."

In my excitement, I gasped for breath and exclaimed, "So are you Sri Guru Babaji's disciple?"

"That is my good fortune," he said calmly. "Now, I would want you to leave and come back tomorrow at the same time and I will tell you about my meeting with Sri Guru Babaji and how he bestowed his grace on me and accepted me as his disciple."

* * * * *

At dawn the next morning, I walked up again to the *kutir* eager to hear what he had to say especially regarding Sri Guru Babaji. He gave me a cup of hot tea in a clay cup brought by an attendant of his.

"Isn't the Ganga beautiful at this time of the day?" he said. I agreed and said, "Please baba, tell me if you can about your meeting with Sri Guru Babaji."

He looked across the river and it looked as if he was reliving the past. "I was then a monk, belonging to the orthodox *Dasanami* order, sitting here in this very place. This was long before I built the *kutir*. I was gazing at the flowing river and contemplating on the vast expansiveness called the *Brahman*. This had been my pratice for many days. I would leave the ashram and spend the whole evening meditating."

"Overcome by an intense desire to renounce everything including the insignia of the order I belonged to, I walked down the steps of the ghat and floated my *dandi* (staff) into the river and watched it float away. My heart was filled with a sense of relief and tranquility as if I had unburdened myself of the last vestige of attachment to the world. I climbed up the steps and, sitting in *sukhasana*, entered the stillness of deep meditation.

When I opened my eyes, I realised that it was probably quite late at night. Everything was still around me; even the boat men seemed to have gone home. The light of a half moon illuminated the river. I stood up and for the first time realised that I was homeless. I could certainly not go back to the monastery, minus my *dandi*."

"I walked aimlessly towards the Dasashwamedha ghat. On the way, I passed the Harishchandra ghat, which apart from Manikarnika ghat, is one place where dead bodies are cremated. As I passed, I looked toward a funeral pyre and saw a dark and dirty man, one of the many attendants of the cremation grounds, considered outcastes by the orthodox, poking the pyre with a long stick, probably trying to make sure that the corpse was burnt uniformly."

"The thought crossed my mind that the fellow would probably be drunk and what a miserable life he led and how unclean he was. All of a sudden, the uncouth attendant looked at me and shouted loudly in a drunken voice, 'Oh maharaj run, I am going to pollute you.' Then holding the stick in his hands, he pranced up the steps and came close to me.

He was laughing wildly and I could smell the alcohol. I did the only thing I could have done, and I ran. There was no one else in sight. The man did not give up; he was chasing me, swinging the stick in his right hand. Breathless, with the fellow still in tow and thinking what a crazy thing to happen, I ran as fast as I could hoping to reach Dasashwamedha. Perhaps I would find someone there, who would save me from the situation."

"Just then, two or three stray dogs joined the chase, barking and trying to snap at my heels. It looked as if they were his companions. As the Dasashwamedha ghats came into sight, one of the mongrels – a large, fierce looking black dog – jumped right across my path. I stumbled and fell on my face, felt a sharp pain on my right eyebrow and I knew I had probably cut myself."

"I was surprised that there were no more barks and snarls and everything was silent, but the fear that the man from the ghats would pounce on me, caused me to shiver uncontrollably. I was afraid to turn and look or get up. I then heard this clear and melodious voice saying, 'Namo Narayana, get up swami, you are in safe hands'."

"With great hesitation, I turned my face and sat up. In front of me stood a bare-bodied, beauteous looking yogi with long brown hair flowing down his shoulders. He was smiling as he said, 'you gave up your dandi, but the feelings of caste and creed, high and low, clean and dirty, have not left your mind, just like the founder of the ancient order of sanyasins, Adi Shankara, who was revolted at seeing an Aghori with his dogs coming close to him. You too feared that the attendant from the Harishchandra Ghat might pollute you by close proximity'."

"There is no untouchable; there are no dogs, all that was conjured up by me. My abode is in Kailash, some call me Sri Guru Babaji. For the first time in your many lives, you are coming in contact with me. I see your inner potential and tonight, I shall accept you as my disciple and teach you the ancient science of kriya referred to by Sri Krishna in the Bhagavad Gita. Wash the wound on your head with the waters of the Ganga and come with me."

"I have no words to explain the state I was in, except to say I was stunned. We walked back to the Assi Ghat. Babaji stood on the steps and shouted loudly '*Aaho!*' thrice. A small boat appeared with a boat man whose face was completely covered in a white cloth except for his eyes."

"'Come' said Babaji and we stepped into the boat. In a short time, we had crossed the Ganga and gone to the sandy shore on the other side. There in complete solitude, Babaji initiated me into the pratice of *kriya* with *mahamudra*, *nabhi kriya* and the *hung sau* technique. That day I had the best meditation. When dawn was approaching and the rising sun began to paint the sky golden, Babaji gestured that we should go back."

"We got into the waiting boat and in a few minutes were back in Assi Ghat. Babaji's parting instuctions were, 'you may continue to wear the ochre robes. Go to Badrinath and for the next year and a half settle down in a *kutir* on the banks of the Alakananda, practise your *kriya* for one hour every day and increase it every week by an hour, until you are able to practice eight hours every day. I shall not see you till the end of your one and a half years of solitude. Come back to Benaras then and I shall review your practice at midnight on the Manikarnika Ghat. Meanwhile, take the vow of *mauna* and to sustain your body take *bhiksha* everyday from the *annachatras* of Badrinath. Have no friends; do not pick up an acquaintance with anybody. I shall myself see that you are given a *kutir*. Have no worry, all your needs will somehow be provided'."

The great yogi then looked at me and said, "that is my story of meeting with Sri Guru Babaji. The next time I met him was at Manikarnika Ghat at midnight as promised by him, after I returned to Benaras from my *sadhana*. Today, I don't stay for more than two months in one place. Somehow, my meagre needs are looked after. It has been six years since I have been practising *kriya yoga*. Certain changes have taken place in my psyche but I still have a long way to go."

"My advice to you is to continue your practice diligently, according to the instructions given to you by Maheshwarnath Babaji. May Sri Guru's blessings be with you." He stopped and blessed me with his hand on my head and said, "Now you can go. You won't see me here tomorrow for I am planning to move. Probably, Sri Guru had some reason to send you to me. I am inspired to advise you to read carefully the *Siddha Siddhanta Paddhati* of Sri Gorakhnath. *Hari Om.*" There was nothing I could do except prostrate and leave. Next day, I went back to Delhi.

13. Facets of Tantra

The following chapter is based on a conversation I had with Maheshwarnath Babaji. Tantra is a word that fascinates many and the interpretations are myriad. I am going to state what I have understood from Babaji.

Tantra is a term used for a certain approach to the Truth. It makes use of *Yantras* which are diagrams, blueprints of the actual mechanics of achieving the results. Tantra believes in the dictum *Bhogo Yogayathe*, which means Yoga or union with the Divine through *Bhoga* (enjoyment or indulgence). It is because of this that many conclude that Tantra is the practice of midnight drunken orgies, where sex is freely indulged in. However, this is far from the truth, although I cannot deny that certain degraded sects do indulge in such activities and consider these activities to be the be all and end all of Tantra.

The truth is that Tantra is a very practical approach to reach that which the Upanishads describe as the 'immeasurable', 'ungraspable' Brahman. Whilst the path of renunciation prescribes total abstinence and severe austerities, tantra teaches that since this path of abstinence can only be practised by a few rare souls there is an alternate approach meant for people who live in this world, who are not monks or renunciants and still aspire to rise to higher planes of existence.

While Vedanta deals with abstract, imperishable, formless Brahman, Tantra deals with the concrete, gross world, tangible to the senses to start with. It leads the aspirant step by step from gross to the subtle, yet tangible, experiences to finer states of consciousness till finally the mind in its extremely subtle and tranquil state is able to grasp the ungraspable.

The true Tantra Yogi believes that all desires – to achieve, expand, enjoy, acquire are all the outward manifestations of the inner urge to reach the total fulfilment and unending Bliss of the Supreme Truth, which may be called Brahman or Shivam. Even when someone drinks, it is for a temporary slowing down of brain activity and the resultant feeling of enjoyable expansiveness. Of course, the core characteristics of an individual are brought to the surface, because of the temporary suspension of inhibitions.

It is said that once Sri Ramakrishna Paramahansa was travelling in a buggy on the streets of Calcutta, when he saw a drunken man laughing and reeling on the footpath. He stopped the carriage, got out and embraced the man saying that he was his drunken brother. Both were drunk he said, himself and the man on the footpath, both were in Bliss and oblivious of the world. 'I am a drunkard too', he said, 'though I drink a different brew.'

It is on record that when bells, which were part of the evening service at the temple of Mother Kali, were rung, Sri Ramakrishna's eyes would go red and he would reel like a drunkard.

Tantra is divided by some writers into the Left and Right hand paths, but Babaji taught me that the distinction is unjustified. It is better to consider *Samaya* or the right hand path as the culmination of the *Vamachara*, also called *Kaulachara*, the left hand path when the mind has become sufficiently purified.

Therefore, the *Pancha Makaras* – the five indulgences, prescribed for the *kaulamargin* which include *Madhu* (wine) and *Maithuna* (sexual union) are used only as stepping stones by the category of practioners called *pashu* (animal like) and *vina* (herd like) respectively. One had to merely mention wine (*madhu*) and Sri Ramakrishna would enter into a trance, a *samadhi*, which often gave the impression to the uninitiated that he was drunk on alcohol, whilst in reality, he was inebriated by the inner nectar which only a yogi can taste.

Let's take *maithuna* (sexual union) the ritualistic practice of which has earned a bad name for the *vamacharins*. Why is it that sexual indulgence is the greatest of enjoyments for most human beings, something for which even heinous crimes are committed? The reason is that the state nearest to the thoughtless tranquility of *samadhi* is experienced by the ordinary human being only during the act. One forgets one's ego consciousness and for a split second even the awareness of the outside world disappears, of course to reappear the next minute in all its imperfections.

Now, even that physical act, performed under controlled conditions, guided by a proper teacher of Tantra can lead to higher states of consciousness through the practice of *vajroli* and shifting attention to the upper phases of the body called the *chakras*. Once the greater bliss of the higher centres is experienced, the physical sex is no longer a priority. *Mait-*

huna has merely become a stepping stone to higher levels of Being.

Libido is also linked to the energy *shakti* or *kulakundalini*, which according to Tantra lies in its potential form coiled like a snake at rest, at the bottom of the spine in the centre called the *muladhara* chakra in all human beings. *Kulakundalini* or *Kundalini* as it is called, is central to the teachings of Tantra and Yoga. Both the yogi and the trantric attempt to awaken this energy in different ways and cause it to ascend through the *sushumna nadi* or channel that lies inside the spinal cord, until it reaches the highest centre on the crown of the head called the *sahasrara* chakra or 'thousand petalled lotus' also called the *sahasrara padma*.

There the union of *kundalini shakti* and the essence of consciousness called *Sada Shiva* takes place. The transcendental ecstasy that the yogi enjoys when this happens is the state known as *samadhi*. The great Adi Shankara, in his work called the *Saundarya Lahiri*, refers to this celebration as the 'Ecstasy of Supreme Beauty.'

On the way to the highest centres, the *kundalini* passes through five chakras on the *sushumna* and new horizons and dimensions are opened to the yogi. The subtle part of his mind expands and he finds himself in possession of powers and capacities which an ordinary man would consider extraordinary.

When the female principle called the *kundalini* merges with the male principle called *Shivam*, the yogi becomes divine, the next step in evolution for human beings. The difference in the evolutionary scale between an evolved yogi who has reached the higher state of consciousness and one who has not is similar to that of the great apes to human beings.

Now the tantric approach to the awakening of the *kundalini*, in contrast to the yogic techniques, makes use of the great *Sri Vidya* mantra – both of the fifteen-letter variety called the *panchadasaksari* and the sixteen-letter one called the *shodasaksari* – and involves external worship of the *yantra* called the *Sri Chakra*, which is later internalised in the heart chakra and finally in the crown chakra.

Babaji, in his infinite kindness, taught me a well balanced combination of Tantric and Yogic techniques, the effectiveness of which I can vouch for.

The chakras starting from the lowest are:
the *muladhara*, at the end of the spine;
the *swadisthana*, just above the reproductive organs;
the *manipura*, at the navel;
the *anahata* at the centre of the chest;
the *vishudha* in the throat;
the *sahasrara* at the crown of the head.

The great *Gorakshnatha* adds two more centres: one at the epiglottis and the other at the centre of the forehead.

The following is all that I can add regarding the information on the chakras for the uninitiated. From the lowest chakra to the highest, the colours to be contemplated upon are yellow, silver, fire red, sky blue, indigo and milk white.

The symbols are a triangle with the apex downwards, a silver crescent moon, a red triangle with apex upwards, a star made of two equilateral triangles interlaced like the star of David, an oval, white two-petalled lotus and multi-coloured lotus.

The seed sounds (*beejaksharas*) that activate the centres starting from the bottom are *lam, vam, ram, yam, ham* and *Om.*

The rest has to be learnt personally from a teacher. How is *Kriya Yoga* connected to all this, I shall describe in the chapter on *Kriya Yoga.*

14. Conversations with Babaji – 1

It was a cold Himalayan night. Babaji and I sat facing each other on a large flat boulder in front of Mouni Baba's cave. Around us, the silvery snowclad ranges glowed in celestial light. Inspite of the crackling fire we had made earlier and the thick blankets wrapped around me, I would shiver when the icy wind blew across my face. Babaji presented an utter contrast to my swaddled and cocooned form, as he sat there bare-bodied save for a single knee length cotton loin cloth tied across his waist. He had mastered the yogic technique of adjusting his body temperature. Sitting in *padmasana*, on the folded woollen blanket, he looked at me with a kind smile.

"Relax," he said. "Be comfortable." His words acted as magic and my tired body, felt miraculously revived. Soothing warmth flowed from him to me, permeating my whole body. My mind became alert with an acuteness I never knew I possessed.

M: Babaji, I have been reading Vedantic subjects for some time now. When I began, I thought I understood everything, but as years passed and I went deeper into the subject, I began to realise how little I had grasped. There are so many questions that have remained unclear. Please unravel the mystery of this statement made in the *Isha Upanishad* – *Andham tamah pravishanti ye avidyaam upaasate tato bhooya iva te tamo ya u vidyaayaam rataah* – 'They who worship ignorance enter into darkness and they who worship knowledge enter into greater darkness.' The first part is clear. We have always been taught from childhood that ignorance is to be overcome by acquiring knowledge, so it is quite baffling to hear the *rishi* say that to worship knowledge is to enter into greater darkness. How can this be? If both ignorance and knowledge lead to darkness, is there something beyond both knowledge and ignorance? If knowledge also leads to darkness, is there something beyond knowledge and ignorance?

Babaji: Now be alert, son. To be alert is not to strain but to relax and let the teachings sink deep so that you will have no more doubts. Listen carefully and after that ask me further questions, if you have any. We will discuss matters as two close friends discuss their personal problems. Let us have complete love and frankness between us. Yes, many have been perplexed by the apparently contradictory statements of the Upanishads. However, if you examine them carefully, there are no contradictions.

They who worship ignorance enter into darkness. Isn't that quite clear? Ignorance, *avidya*, is a lack of knowledge. It is by acquiring knowledge, *jnana*, that ignorance is destroyed. Nowhere does the Upanishad say not to acquire knowledge, for knowledge is the only instrument that can dispel ignorance. Everything that we learn is knowledge, including what you are hearing from me now. Then, how can knowledge lead to darkness? Listen carefully. The Upanishad does not say that knowledge leads to darkness. All it says is that those who worship knowledge enter into greater darkness. This has to be examined closely.

You walked into a field full of thistles and you get a thorn lodged in your foot. You now try to pull it out with your bare hands but to no avail. So you find a sharper, longer, sturdier thorn to remove the one that is lodged. Similarly, you remove the thorn of ignorance and pain with the thorn of knowledge. Tell me, will you after getting rid of the painful thorn, stick the larger thorn into your foot? No you won't. You will throw it away. So it is the thorn of knowledge used for removing the thorn of ignorance. Both of them are discarded by the yogi, the seeker, whose aim is liberation.

Before we go further, let us see what knowledge is. You understand something or an event and say that you have acquired knowledge of that. This means that you have stored all the information or as much as you can with regard that event or thing in your memory. You can now refer back to it, recognise it and react accordingly to it in the future. All knowledge is like that – that which is stored in one's memory.

The moment you have listened to my words, they have vanished from the present and become a thing of the past. They constitute memory and memory is a thing of the past. Knowledge, as we know it, is then something that you remember whether from the recent past or a split second ago or years ago. All knowledge is therefore memory, a thing of the past.

Now, *Brahman*, the ultimate reality is never a memory or a thing of the past. It is the living present, the eternal, immediate present and therefore can never be comprehended by knowledge, which only has the past as reference.

M: If all knowledge is memory, what is it that can know *Brahman*?

Babaji: When the mind, understanding this fact perfectly, gives up all mental effort and becomes quiet and tranquil then all that remain is *Brahman*.

M: Am I then to understand that knowledge, as we generally understand the term, is useless?

Babaji: No, certainly not. The capacity for knowledge, whatever the level of perfection, is the highest faculty of man. Each level in the hierarchy of knowledge I spoke about has its proper place. Without experience derived through our senses, however unreliable or unreal they may be, we cannot comprehend our immediate world of living. However, our reasoning faculty itself can show that reason is often unreliable, coloured as it is by our subjective prejudices.

When the mind, which is nothing more than a collection of thoughts, is transcended, knowledge, which is memory, a thing of the past, comprehends fully how finite it is and therefore how it cannot reach out to the Infinite from which intelligence itself proceeds. Giving up all reasoning, arguments and doubts, the mind, then lets go of the chain of thoughts and becomes as still and placid as an infinite expanse of clear water, without a single ripple on it.

It is in that calm, mirror-like, pure mind that the ultimate, absolute, blissful reality, the *Brahman*, is reflected.

This is what the *Kenopanishad* means when it says: 'That which even the mind cannot reach but because of which the mind acquires the faculty to comprehend; That, O seeker, is the true *Brahman*, nothing that you worship here.'

M: But doesn't the mind become inert like that of an idiot by ceasing to think and reason?

Babaji: How can the mind which reflects the very seed and source of intelligence ever become inert? Such a mind is ever active, ever engaged in doing what has been ordained as its duty. Such a mind, blessed by an abundant rush of energy as it is linked to the very fountainhead of the tremendous energy that operates the entire universe, is not ruffled by obstacles or failures.

It gets neither dejected by failure nor overjoyed by success. It is a mind that works steadily without the distractions that the ordinary person has. It is only such a mind that can be truly said to function, charged as it is with the energy from the Universal Generator. The rest are inert because they have not discovered the secret of work.

Let us look at the minds of some great personalities who were not only thinkers but doers. Adi Shankara was one of the foremost exponents of *Advaita Vedanta* – I shall go into it later – and he was a sanyasin par excellence. In a short span of thirty two years, he did what ordinary people would have taken a hundred years or more to accomplish or perhaps would not even have accomplished in a few lifetimes. He travelled on foot through the length and breadth of this vast country, wrote voluminous commentaries, engaged numerous scholars of the day in debates and renovated temples wherever he went. He was

successful in everything, for he had understood the secret
of work.

Take a more recent example of the great Vedantist Swami
Vivekananda. What a towering personality and what a tire-
less worker for the good of humanity. You, yourself can think
of many examples like these.

M: Babaji, what about those who prefer to remain silent
after realising the Ultimate Truth?

Babaji: If the perfected sage prefers to remain silent, that
silence is more effective than speech or overt action. The sage
works silently on the minds of those who listen to the voice
of silence. Such a sage has reached the source of all thought
and can change the entire world by a single thought. That
silence is more potent than hours of lectures. Silently, such
a sage works miracles, while himself remaining hidden like
the ultimate *Brahman*. By a single thought of such a sage,
Herculean tasks are executed.

Now I will explain another aspect of the statement, 'They
who worship knowledge, enter into greater darkness'. Some
people, when they have studied the scriptures and the numerous commentaries and other branches of Vedic knowledge
like astrology, mathematics, *mantras* and so on, get puffed
with pride, pretending to be learned men.

Their ego is so bloated that they begin to think that they
are always right and refuse to listen to or deign to consider
the other point of view. Their mindset cannot accept that
there may be some other way of looking at the same problem or a differing view point that they might have failed to

grasp. Their excessive pride is invariably the cause of their downfall and their consequent misery.

Their minds lose sensitivity and alertness and are tarnished by dross which they mistake for knowledge, since it has been acquired painstakingly over a long period. They are the worshippers of knowledge who enter into greater darkness.

I shall illustrate what I said by a story. There was a great God-realised saint to whom seekers used to flock. A scholar too went to him for instruction. After listening to the saint for a short while the scholar asked, "How soon can I achieve the liberated state, Sir?" "After a long time," said the teacher.

A poor illiterate gardener, who was also there at that time and was listening to the saint with rapt attention, got up and thanked the saint with folded hands saying, "Sir, I don't know how to thank you for what you have taught. I am an ignorant man. Will I ever attain the highest?" "In a few days," said the teacher.

This answer piqued the scholar. "How is it," he asked, "that this ignoramous can attain the highest in a few days whilst I, a great scholar, shall have to wait for so long?" The saint said quickly, "Your mind is so cluttered up with things that you have collected that it will take a long time for you to unlearn all the misconceptions you have already formed. Your ego is so swollen up that it has shut the door of understanding and simplicity through which Truth enters. The moment you are free of all this rubbish, you will attain the highest. It is to remove all this dirt, that I have given you so much time."

M: Does this mean that the ignorant have more chance to know the Reality than the learned?

Babaji: Certainly not. I was giving you an illustration to show that memorising dozens of texts and scriptures cannot make one learned. A truly learned person is one who has the capacity to grasp and understand and not merely memorise. It is only a mind that is free of misconceptions that can understand – because of its intellectual sharpness – that however high the intellect may soar, it has certain limitations, a certain dimension beyond which it cannot reach.

M: I don't understand clearly what you mean by this dimension beyond.

Babaji: Many people don't. It is difficult for a person who is accustomed to a three dimensional world of length, breadth and depth, whose thoughts are conditioned by these limiting dimensions, to conceive of a 'fourth' dimension beyond the mind itself. It can be experienced only when the entire chain of thoughts, is totally quiet and silent. Only by living in it, can it be understood. But I will try and explain as logically as possible. At least, you will be able to grasp it intellectually and, contemplating upon it, perhaps experience it.

Imagine two wafer thin, red coloured, disc-like creatures living in a large box without a roof. They move on the floor of the box in all directions. They obviously cannot move outside the box because of the walls. Inside the box, they can move along the length and breadth of the box, but not up or down the walls. Having been brought up in that space, they are familiar only with the limited dimensions and height and depth don't exist. They have never ventured out of the square box.

Let us say, someone dips his hands into the box from above and lifts one of them and transfers it to a similar box in which green disc-like creatures live. In the same way a green one is transferred to a red box. Both the green and red creatures are at a loss as to how they were transferred. They cannot conceive of a movement upwards and downwards, since they are used only to lateral movement. For them, any movement other than the horizontal is a miracle and they continue to live in their new environment, aware of only their two dimensional space.

Most of us are like these imagined creatures. We cannot conceive of a dimension other than or higher than, the world of our five senses – sight, sound, touch, smell and taste – where the world of the intellect is itself conditioned by the world of sensory experiences. The spiritual journey begins only when the alert intellect recognises the possibility of another dimension, where it cannot reach by normal means of thought or sensory perception, and starts exploring other means to get there. It is difficult to believe that anyone could have touched this dimension, especially as it is so difficult to visualise.

An adaptation of the story 'Allegory of the Cave' by the Greek philopsopher Plato illustrates the same point. In a long underground tunnel, just wide enough and high enough for a person to stand, moves a line of slaves bound to each other with inter-connected shackles. Their hands, legs and heads are manacled with heavy chains and their heads bowed down with the weight of the chains. They have been there from the time they can remember. They can move only in one direction and they can look only in one direction. For years, they have been walking in a continuous loop in the tunnel.

One of the men is freed by accident though he does not realise this, used as he is to the mechanical and ceaseless movement, until one day, a sharp pain in his neck forces him to turn around and up. He looks up to see a dim light. He walks towards the light, although it dazzles him, and he sees the reality and realises that what he saw in the cave was just a shadow world.

He is the man who has experienced a dimension that is beyond the limited view of those inside the cave. What would be the reaction of his cave mates, if he visited them subsequently and related to them the wonders of a completely different world of light and freedom? They would not be able to grasp the fact that he is telling them the truth. They would be sceptical and call him crazy or a liar, until they themselves became free to experience the world as he has. The man who got free is like the wise sage.

15. Conversations with Babaji – 2

M: I would now like to understand the essence of the *Shanti Mantra* from the same Upanishad.

> *Purnamadah, purnamidam*
> *Purnat purnamudacyate*
> *Purnasya purnamadaya*
> *Purnameva avasisyate*

That is complete, this is complete. From that completeness comes this completeness. When completeness is taken away from completeness, Completeness alone remains.

This is rather confusing and I often wonder whether it is a play on words.

Babaji: No Vedic statement is a mere play on words. The *shanti mantra* you quoted is nothing but the law of 'conservation of energy' as it is now known. As you know, the law of conservation of energy states that energy or its equivalent in mass can neither be created nor destroyed but just changed. It means that nothing can be added or subtracted from it. That completeness is *Brahman*.

Just as this energy can be transformed into another energy, but can neither be created nor destroyed, so also does

Brahman manifest in various forms and cannot be subjected to any addition or destruction.

M: Please, could you explain the saying that the world is unreal. How can the world which is so palpable, which we can see, touch and feel all the time be unreal?

Babaji: It is certainly a very important question. We will look at it from various angles. Let us first consider the question of sight. We see the sun rise and set every day with our own eyes. Does the sun really rise or set? Science tells us that it doesn't, the sun remains stationary and that it is the earth that revolves round it. Against this truth, our eyes tell us something different. Are we then to believe our eyes that the sun rises and sets or believe the evidence of scientific data? Isn't then the information collected by our sense organs often false?

M: Yes, I agree. We can't believe everything we see. Sense perception can be an illusion.

Babaji: We will now analyse why the Vedanta declares the world to be unreal. Everything that exists in this world is constantly in motion. Night gives way to day, life to death and then to new life again. Millions of cells in your body die every minute and new ones take their place. What is here today is not here tomorrow. Can anyone hold on to the present as time speeds on? The moment a thought is born, it has vanished into the past. No ordinary man knows when it all began or when it is going to end, if it ends at all. Can something which appears and vanishes like a bubble, that is not permanent, be real?

Reality is permanent, eternal. Nothing that keeps changing and is temporary can be real. The only unchanging, undecaying reality is *Brahman*. Let us examine the question of the reality of the world governed by senses, more closely. For the purposes of analysis let us consider a small wooden cube painted green. The first characteristic that distinguishes it from other objects is its colour. The light spectrum, the rays emitted by the sun, consists of violet, indigo, blue, green, yellow, orange and red. During our school days, we have seen Newton's disc – a disc painted with these colours, when rotated fast, is seen as white due to the fact that white light is a combination of these colours. We have also seen the alternate, where a beam of white light is refracted through a glass prism, it immediately splits into the seven colours.

Colour then is a function of light. When an object is said to be green, that is not strictly true. What we see as green, is due to the cube absorbing all the colours of the spectrum except green which colour it reflects. Any object that absorbs all the colours and reflects none is black, whilst one that reflects all colours is white. The only quality that any material has by virtue of its molecular structure and chemical composition is that of reflecting certain colours and absorbing others.

What concerns us therefore is the question whether the colour green is a quality or an attribute of the wooden block before us.

M: Yes, I agree that the green colour is not its intrinsic quality or attribute.

Babaji: So, the first attribute, the so-called colour of the object is not really its attribute at all. Colour is not an attribute of any object; it is a function of the light falling on the object. If we were colour blind, then our colour perception is limited. Isn't colour then an illusion?

Let us now consider the shape of the object in our example – a cube. It is an object, contained by six equal squares. When we look at it, we do not see all its sides at the same time. By observing any three sides of it at a time, we decide that it is a cube. What happens is that the rays of light that reflect from the object pass through the lens of the eye and form an image of the object on the retina behind the lens – not the entire image, but one or two or three sides of the object depending on the angle of vision and the size of the object. In spite of this partial data, our brain concludes it to be a cube, unconsciously seeing the other sides beyond our vision. Of course, the entire process takes place in a split second and we call it seeing.

You might have also noticed a contrary phenomenon. If you looked out of a windscreen of a car awash with water, you will see the straight electric posts bent and trees and other objects distorted. Yet another instance of distortion is if you look at a glass plate with an irregular surface, your face may appear as a caricature.

Now, imagine a creature born with eyes of a different structure from those of a human being, it might see things differently and you would not believe it if it told you about its version of shapes such as seeing a straight line as a curve.

M: This uncertainty is only with regard to sight. How about the sense of touch – I would be able to feel the shape of the cube.

Babaji: It is possible that we may be unable to feel all sides of the cube at once, if it were life-size for instance. In this instance, we conclude that it is a cube by a visual perception and partial tactile impression. You must have heard of the famous story of the six blind men and the elephant and how each concluded as to the shape of the elephant.

You can also conduct a practical experiment about your sense of touch. Take two glasses, one with lukewarm water and the other with cold water. Dip the index finger of each hand, one in the lukewarm water and the other in cold water. Take the fingers out and immediately plunge them in the two glasses in reverse order. You will find that the finger plunged from the cold water into the lukewarm water feels that much hotter than previously.

We now know that two of the attributes we thought as intrinsic to the cube are not really its characteristics; the cube has lost its colour and shape. The third attribute that we shall take up now is the size. Size is again a relative concept. Our cube is, let us say, four inches long, four inches broad and four inches high.

The size as seen by the naked eye is purely relative. If you look at it from afar, it might appear smaller than when seen from up close. Imagine a tiny creature like an ant facing the cube, it would see a block of formidable proportions. For us a grain of sugar is miniscule but to the ant which carries it, it might be a big weight. Yet again, a child sees her father as a giant when she is little, but not so when she grows up. Size is also relative and depends on the observer.

Now where is the cube with its commonly acknowledged attributes? What is its real size? Is it big, small or tiny? There are no definite answers.

M: What about mass? It is solid, I can feel it.

Babaji: Imagine a microscopic organism that enters your body. It is so tiny, that the pores of your skin are large gates through which it enters with ease. For it, your blood stream is probably a flowing river and arteries and veins, huge tunnels. Your solid body is not solid for the organism that is smaller than a single cell.

Let us look at solidity from another angle. As you know, all so-called solid matter contains primarily of atoms bound together by empty space. You cannot see this empty space with your naked eye. The magnified image under the microscope shows the solid matter for what it is.

Let us go a little further. What is the atom? It is a central nucleus around which electrons revolve like planets in the solar system. The nucleus and the electrons occupy very little space in the total area of the atom. The protons and neutrons that constitute the nucleus can be further split into mesons and other sub-atomic particles.

So where is the thing that you called solid? Our *rishis*, who delved deep into these subjects by virtue of their special faculties, have found that matter is ultimately simply a field in which different forces act and react.

With one more example, we shall dismiss the notion of solidity. A piece of cloth is impenetrable to the pressure of your finger, you can't push your finger through it unless the cloth is very old or you tear it. Under a magnifying glass, however, you will see the same piece of cloth as having many spaces between the warp and weft. A microscopic creature can easily pass through these. To that creature, it is not solid and impenetrable but a vast space with no obstructions at all. Isn't mass relative?

Finally, let's consider the weight of the cube. The concept of weight can be demolished fairly easily. Weight is nothing but the gravitational force exerted by the earth. That explains why things start floating when they are away from gravity. Weight then, is also relative.

There are multiple examples that can be discussed. Isn't it sufficiently clear by now that what we take for granted as reality of objects or the infallibility of our sensory perceptions, is an illusion, a construct of mind, our thoughts and our feelings?

This is not to deny the existence of objects or our ability to comprehend them. What is to be understood is that the world is real only in a relative way but it cannot be real in the absolute sense. Relative reality is essential only as far as it concerns our functioning in the world; no more no less. Unfortunately, to accept relative reality as the absolute reality is the error we fall into and therein lies all our misery.

Since you have a scientific bent of mind, I shall compare the need to accept the relative reality of the world with that of accepting Newtonian laws to explain many phenomena in the visible world or at the atomic level. But when we consider the same laws at the sub-atomic level, these are found to be inadequate.

The modern mind is very much inclined to dismiss what our ancient sages and saints stated about the insubstantiality of the world. However, today's science is inclined to accept it. Otherwise why would the physicist Arthur Stanley Eddington say, "Our conception of substance is only vivid so long as we do not face it"? It begins to fade when we analyse it. We may dismiss many of its supposed attributes which are evidently projections of our sense-impressions outwards into the external world.

Thus the colour which is so vivid to us is in our minds and cannot be embodied in a legitimate conception of the substantial object itself. But in any case, colour is no part of the essential nature of substance. Its supposed nature is that which we try to call to mind by the word "concrete", which is perhaps an outward projection of our sense of touch.

It is this uncertainty about the actual nature of the objective world that is termed as the great illusion. Only the mere existence of it can be acknowledged, not the form in which it appears to exist. The absolute reality behind these illusions might appear abstract, but it is only abstract in the sense that it is beyond the reach of our sense conditioned to the practical, yet illusory, needs of our day-to-day world.

According to the sages, this abstractness called *Brahman* is the only true reality, the only true existence. Our intellect can go a step further than our sense only to acknowledge and understand that the *Brahman* cannot be intellectually grasped. That pure existence, behind the insubstantiality of the world and constantly changing forms, is realized only in deep meditation, beyond the intellect and the mind, when thoughts have completely ceased.

16. The Great Avadhuta Sadashiva Brahmendra

In the 18th century, I was born as one of the important *begums* in the harem of a Muslim ruler, the *Nawab* of a small principality in the Arcot province in South India. It was then that I came into contact in a very strange manner with the great yogi and *avadhuta* Sadashiva Brahmendra. May the dust of his feet be forever on my head.

Before I begin my story, let me introduce you to the great one. Roughly 300 years ago, Somasundara Avadhaani, a Brahmin from Andhra Pradesh, lived in Madurai with his wife Parvati. Somasundara was a scholar and a practitioner of *Kundalini Yoga*, and was acknowledged as a yogi by his contemporaries. His wife Parvati desired to have a child who would be a great soul – a *satputra*.

On the advice of her husband, she undertook the chanting of the *Rama Nama* tens of millions of times until it was said her mind continued to chant even in sleep. At Rameswaram, while on a pilgrimage, both of them dreamt that Shiva, the Lord of Rameswaram blessed them and announced that a *satputra* would be born as their son. On returning to Madurai, a son was born to them – a very handsome boy who they named Sivaramakrishnan.

A child prodigy, Sivaramakrishnan quickly narrated the *sastras*. His teachers thought that he was merely revising the knowledge he had acquired in a previous life and introduced him to the great Sridhara Venkatesa Ayyaval popularly known as Ayyaval of Tiruvisanallur.

Meanwhile, his mother arranged marriage for him since his father had left for the Himalayas to perform penance. Not wanting to hurt her feelings, he agreed and at the age of twelve was married to a girl of five as was the custom in those days. The bride was then taken to her parents' home to grow up before she could be brought back to her marital home. Sivaramakrishnan continued to be deeply immersed in his studies and spiritual pursuits as if nothing had happened.

Ayyaval, seeing him enter into spiritual trances frequently, entrusted him to the care of the great scholar, sage and yogi, Sri Paramashivendra. Directed by his guru Sri Paramashivendra, Sivaramakrishnan became the *Sansthana Vidwan* of the Maharaja of Mysore. After sometime, he became disillusioned by life in Mysore and summoned by his guru he returned. Sivaramakrishnan prostrated at his feet and sat silently. Referring to his having defeated many a Vedic scholar during Vedantic discussions in the Mysore Palace and having rendered them speechless, Sri Paramashivendra said to him, "you have learnt to tie up the tongues of others but you haven't learnt to shut up yourself."

Taking that as a spirutal instruction, Sivaramakrishnan stopped talking and became a *mouni*. Sri Paramashivendra conferred sanyas, ordained him as a renunciant, named him Sadashiva and told him to perform *tapasya* (intense spiritual practice) at any place he liked. Sadashiva came to Nerur, which even today is a solitary and beautiful spot on the banks of the river Cauvery, surrounded by mountains and abundant greenery. There he remained absorbed in the bliss of the Supreme Brahman.

Sometimes he would wander about and come back when he pleased. He had become an *avadhuta*, a free spirit, one with the blissful *Brahman*, a naked saint without even a loincloth, going where he pleased, not tied down by norms laid down by society. Many wonderful stories are told about his life.

Near Kodamundi, jutting out like an island from the Cauvery river, there existed a big rock called the Agastya Parai. To remain isolated, Sadashiva Brahman as he was called, used to sit on the rock and meditate for ten to fifteen days at a stretch. Once the river flooded and he was carried away by the swirling waters and buried in the river-bed. Sadashiva Brahman was in a deep trance. Many months later, labourers who had come to collect sand were shocked to see blood oozing from a spot where they were digging, when their spades hit something soft.

With the arrival of the village head, the sand was carefully excavated and they discovered the body of Sadashiva Brahman still in *samadhi*. When his body was warmed up by massaging and making him drink hot porridge, Sadashiva woke up from the trance and quietly walked away.

Once, in the Tiruvarangkulam forests of the Kingdom of Puddukottai he was found under a huge quantity of hay where he had fallen whilst in a trance. When the upper layers of the haystack were used as feed for the buffaloes, the farmers found Sadashiva's body at the bottom. Sadashiva woke up and quickly walked away. He had been buried in the haystack for over a year. Informed by the minister of this, the Maharaja of Puddukottai, Vijaya Raghunatha Thondaiman who was a scholar and loved saints and sadhus, sought out and found Sadashiva in an isolated spot. After offering his prostrations, he begged Sadashiva to grace the palace. Sadashiva said nothing and continued to meditate.

The Maharaja himself built a hut nearby and engaged himself in the service of the great sage. For short periods, he would go to the palace, attend to his duties and come back. Seven years passed and one day, Thondaiman pleaded with Sadashiva to initiate him into a mantra. Sadashiva wrote the mantra in sand. The king is said to have collected the sand, on which the *Dakshinamurthy mantra* was written, in his own *angavastra* (upper cloth), and took it to the palace, placed it in a gold box and commenced the practice of performing *puja* daily.

It is also said and authenticated by many that once when Sadashiva Brahman was walking in a flower garden at Karur, the little children who always gathered around him and considered him as one of them, expressed a strong desire to go and see the Madurai temple festival.

Sadasiva told them to climb on his back and close their eyes. Lo and behold, they were enjoying the festival and feasting their eyes on Lord Sundareswarar, a form of Shiva being taken in a procession. Then he got them tasty sweets and brought them back the same way. The parents were relieved that their missing children had come back and were astonished to hear what had happened. The children even shared the leftover sweets, which were available only in Madurai. Some parents felt sad that they had not got the same opportunity as their dear children.

In another instance, the watchmen guarding the paddy fields of a rich *zamindar* were rendered statue like with their hands aloft, when they tried to assault Sadashiva mistaking him to be a thief. Only after Sadashiva walked quite a distance, did they regain their mobility.

*****

There are innumerable stories of Sri Sadashiva Brahman and his astounding powers, but let me now come back to my personal experience. As I said at the beginning of this chapter, around three hundred years ago, I was born in the South Arcot district as the favourite *begum* of the *Nawab*, who was a vassal to the Nawab of Arcot. His harem had over twenty *begums* but he loved me the most. I was the daughter of an Afghan nobleman and was called Moti (pearl).

The *Nawab* enjoyed undressing me in a private tent in the harem, enjoying my nakedness, decorating me with jewels, anklets and anointing me with *attar*. One day while he was engaged in doing this, the tent flap that covered the entrance of the tent, flew open and in walked a strange, tall and handsome man. His bearded face was illumined with a divine glow and his eyes were dancing with joy as if he was enjoying something secret, not attainable by ordinary mortals. He was stark naked.

He looked at the *Nawab* and then at me. Our eyes met. Something like a cool breeze entered my eyes and went into my heart. My heart was filled with bliss and I felt like a mother ready to embrace her child. I stood frozen with love. The *Nawab* overcame his initial shock. He was livid. He called the guards who came running, but wonder of wonders, they could not see him. Only the two of us could.

The *Nawab* drew his sword and in great anger cut off Sadashiva's right arm at the shoulder. The severed arm fell down and blood flowed copiously from the stump. The strange being laughed joyously, turned and walked out of the tent.

"What have you done?" I screamed turning to the *Nawab*. "That was the great *mastan*, the Hindu holyman, we have been hearing about for sometime now. He is not conscious of his body and it does not matter to him if he is clothed or not. Run my king, run to him, find him and seek his pardon for this heinous crime. In his infinite kindness, he might forgive you. Allah is compassionate and merciful. Go."

My husband was shivering with fear and remorse. He picked up the severed arm and ran out of the tent. I fell unconscious. When I came back to consciousness, I saw the *Nawab* sitting beside me. He was calm and his demeanour was peaceful. He then told me what had happened.

He said that he had run behind the saint, holding the severed arm for a long distance, before he entered a forest and sat on a rock. There the *Nawab* prostrated at his feet and cried for foregiveness. The saint said that he had committed no sin. The *Nawab* showed him the severed arm, whereupon the saint merely stuck it back to his shoulder and the wound healed instantaneously.

"It's all fine now," he said to my husband. "Now, hand over the kingdom to your successor and go to Karachi. You have a spark of spiritual yearning in you. In Karachi, lives a great Sufi incognito. You will recognise him. Become his disciple and live there all your life. Tell him I send him blessings and that I will grant his prayer and appear in Karachi before him when I release my body. He should keep the burial pit ready for me. As for that pearl (*moti*) of yours, she is one of us. I came to re-awaken the flame of her spiritual aspiration which was on the verge of being snuffed out."

"She will be absorbed more and more in the bliss of the Inner Being. She will die on the same day that I give up my body at Nerur. Tell her, I will bless her soul, which will come to pay obeisance to me when I discard my physical body. She shall then be born as a male in a learned and pure Brahmin family, which would have migrated from Benaras and settled down in a village near Badrinath."

"There she will become like her father, a disciple of the great Sri Guru, who is a manifestation of Adinath and who lives in the Himalayas. Due to a certain deed, she will again be born as a male in a Muslim family down south in the land of Shankara, where she will be contacted by a senior disciple of Sri Guru. It is only in that life, that the soul will be finally liberated after all its *vasanas* are burnt away. Go now. Make haste."

Within a week, the *Nawab* handed over his kingdom to one of his sons and quietly slipped away one night from his kingdom, clad in a fakir's robes. I suffered a lot under the new dispensation. Years later, I became seriously ill and as I lay on my death bed I had a vision of the Lord of my soul Sri Sadashiva Brahman who said, "leave your body now and come to Nerur. I am relinquishing my physical body. Your husband will also see me in Karachi."

The body lay dead and I saw myself travelling in the air to a beautiful wooded place with a river flowing nearby. I guessed it was Nerur. There, I saw my Lord enter the pit they had prepared for him. There were hundreds of people, kings and commoners. In the midst of that crowd, his compassionate eyes fell on this insignificant soul standing nearby, invisible to others. He raised his right hand in my direction and blessed me. I then got sucked into a tunnel of light and my memories got wiped out temporarily. It was as if I was entering deep sleep.

* * * * *

The *Mahasamadhi* of Sri Sadashiva Brahmendra is in Nerur not far from Karur in Tamilnadu. A big *Bilva* tree, which as foretold by the great saint sprouted from the *samadhi* on the ninth day, stands even today. Twelve feet away is a Shiva *linga* brought from Kashi by a *Brahmachari* and installed twelve days after his *Mahasamadhi*, just as predicted by him.

My soul is bathed in bliss and splendour whenever I go to Nerur and sit near the *samadhi*. The *samadhi* reverberates with his presence. This is the first time I have revealed my humble past connection with the loving, merciful, compassionate Sadashiva who is always merged in the Supreme *Brahman*.

17. The Kutir at Rudraprayag

In May 2012, I led a group of friends numbering around
one hundred and sixty to the snowy Himalayan shrines
of Kedarnath and Badrinath. It was a large and motley
group of new and old friends. What kept them together was
the spirit of pilgrimage to the ancient snow-clad mountains.
Her Highness Bhavanidevi Hemant Singh of Dolhpur, who
I in a lighter vein call *Maha Mandaleshwar*, ably assisted
by Kanwaljit Singh of Skylark Travels, managed the difficult
job of keeping together such a disparate group and making
the trip a great success. When we started out from Delhi,
there were thirty eight Toyota Innovas with Satsang Foundation banners, numbered one to thirty eight. We came back in
the same order without even a puncture.

On the way back from Kedar, we drove down to
Rudraprayag and stayed over for the night before setting
out the next day for Badrinath. Some of us were staying at
the Monal Resort Hotel.

After a wash, I opened the back door of my room and
stood surveying the scene from the balcony. Down below,
flowed the sacred river Ganga, formed by the confluence of
the Alaknanda and Mandakini. Her voice was a gentle roar,
feminine yet firm and mighty. I could see the bathing ghat and
a little above, the roof of the tiny old temple dedicated to the
goddess Bhadrakali, a wrathful manifestation of the Supreme

energy. With my heart full of joy, I locked the room and came down to the garden and walked behind the resort. A small door opened out of the compound wall. I went out of the door and walked down the hill, until I reached the temple. What I was looking for was a *kutir*, a yogi's hut that existed near the temple many years ago when there was no resort or hotel and one could walk down the road to the *kutir*. Steps from the *kutir* led to the river. Yes, the *kutir* was there, now a *pucca* one, built of brick and mortar. I knew that the yogi, whom I had once met during my blissful wandering days with Babaji, had passed away. He had belonged to the *Nath sampradaya* (tradition) and was known as Badranath.

In 1990, five years after Babaji's *samadhi*, I had gone on my annual travels in the Himalayas and had spent some time in this *kutir* with another sadhu. He called himself Ananda. In 1996, I received a letter from him saying that he was going to the upper Himalayas and would probably not return. I was curious. Would there be another yogi or sanyasin in the *kutir*?

I did not have to wait for long. On a platform under the huge *Peepal* tree sat a sadhu with matted hair. "*Har Har Mahadev*" he greeted me. "*Shambho Mahadev*," I replied. He was not meditating or studying or chanting. He was powdering charas and preparing his chillum (clay pipe) for a smoke.

"Please join me," he said. "Some more friends will come soon. This is excellent stuff from Nepal." I declined.

"How long have you been here?"

"More than a year," he said. "People like you give me money so I can buy provisions and cook some food for myself. The villagers no longer give food to sadhus. I go up to the town to buy things."

As I turned to go down the river, lamenting the state of affairs in the sacred Himalayas where drug addicts called themselves holy men and the real yogis are rare to find, he called out to me.

"Please give me some money, *sarkar.*"

I gave him a hundred rupees, as I would have given to any beggar who pleaded for help and quickly walked away down to the river. Dusk was approaching and I could see two of the group, C.V. Ramnath and Shanthan, standing on the banks of the river. I sat on a rock overlooking the river and listened to the song of the flowing waters.

My thoughts first went to the night I spent with Babaji and yogi Badranathji at the *kutir.* That was not an eventful stay except that the next morning Babaji and Badranathji had a good laugh saying that I had snored louder than the snort of a wild boar. The next morning, we had left for Guptakashi.

Then in 1990, as I mentioned previously, I met sadhu Ananda. It is about this meeting and the ten days that I spent with sadhu Ananda that I will now elaborate upon.

* * * * *

This time around I was not the *parivrajaka* (wandering sadhu) of the early days. My hair was cropped in the so-called civilized mode and I wore jeans and a t-shirt. I carried a rucksack and travelled by bus, jeep, car or whatever transport was available. I was not bare-foot, I wore canvas shoes.

One evening, I got off the bus at Rudraprayag and walked to the *kutir* beside the river. The Monal Resort had not come up as yet. By the time I reached the place it was getting dark. With the help of my flashlight, I made my way down the road and reached the *kutir*. I walked up to the door. The *kutir* was lit by the dim light of a kerosene lamp. The *dhuni* outside was still smouldering. Someone came out and it was not Badranathji, who used to live there. This was a middle-aged man in a white kurta and dhoti.

"*Namaste,*" I said.

"*Namaste,* come in," he said in English.

Once inside the *kutir*, he bade me unload the rucksack off my shoulder. I sat down and made myself comfortable. The bearded, long-haired and tall resident of the *kutir* introduced himself as *sadhu* Ananda, originally from Tamil Nadu, who had occupied the *kutir* after the passing away of the Nath *sadhu* Badranathji, whom he had stayed with for two years. Badranathji had gone off to Benaras on a pilgrimage and had given up his body there voluntarily, by walking into the river Ganga.

When I introduced myself, he said he had heard of Maheshwarnath Babaji and me. He cordially invited me to stay as long as I wanted. Food was no problem as he had independent financial resources and bought all his provisions from the town. He would, of course, be happy if I helped him with the cooking, which was done on the kerosene stove he had. I accepted his offer and stayed on for ten days.

We went for long walks, bathed in the Ganga, meditated and discussed religion and philosophy seriously. He was well-travelled, well-read, educated and taken to the life of a *sadhu* after weighing all options. A graduate from the prestigious Indian Institute of Technology, Delhi, he had taught physics in a prestigious U.S university for seven years before deciding to return to India and become a spiritual seeker. He was single and had no connection with his family; a soft-spoken, good natured and extremely intelligent man. I thoroughly enjoyed and greatly benefited by being with him for those ten days. After Babaji, it was Ananda who suggested that I write about my experiences.

I shall now recount one of the most extra-ordinary experiences he said he had had.

"One evening," he said, "I was sitting beside the Ganga near the *kutir*, in a very depressed mood. I had met many sadhus, read quite a bit of the religious and mystical teachings of not only the Hindus, but also other religions and had been practising different kinds of meditation for over eight years."

"None of the sadhus I met came up to my expectations and I refused to accept them as my gurus. Having read J. Krishnamurti extensively, I sort of endorsed his opinion that a guru was not required and may even turn out to be an obstacle. My meditation, although quite inspiring in the beginning, was now insipid and mechanical. There was no joy."

"I was racked by severe doubts and even began to wonder if this whole thing called 'spiritual seeking' was a waste of time and energy, invented by lazy bums and ganja addicts who misguided young and sensitive minds. I said to myself that it was time to abandon this futile way of life and go back to the plains. With my qualifications, I was sure, I could land a teaching job in a university and lead a normal life; perhaps get married, for my attraction to the opposite sex continued to be strong, in spite of my self-imposed celibacy."

"Despite all this, I could not draw my mind away from the flowing river and the grandeur of the mountains and the simple life of a sadhu. Tortured by conflicting thoughts and totally confused, I held my head in my hands and with closed eyes hailed loudly—Where are the masters who are said to dwell in the Himalayas? Why do they not come to the help of a sincere and tortured soul like me? Is it all a myth to fool the innocent?"

"I cried my heart out. I then felt someone touch my right shoulder softly. I opened my eyes. Beside me stood a shrivelled old man who was bare-bodied except for a yellow loin cloth. He had a thin long face, sparsely bearded, with eyes sunk deep in their sockets. He wore the paraphernalia of a *Vaishnavite Bairagi*, a large U shaped mark, drawn in sandalwood paste on his forehead, *tulsi* beads on his neck and similar sandalwood paste markings on his chest and upper arms. His hair was matted, brownish-black, tied up in a large bun. He was bare foot and carried a brass water pot."

"I bowed down, touched his feet as is the custom and said *Hari Om*."

"In a slightly feminine, soothing yet firm voice, he said, 'Don't give up so easily, son. It takes many lives on this path. Strive and you shall see the light. Teaching jobs in colleges are not so difficult to get, but a seeker's life is priceless and doesn't come to all and sundry'."

"I was stunned, not because he seemed to have read my mind, a feat I have seen many sadhus do, but at the timing of his arrival. 'Are you one of the Himalayan masters, *Swami*'? I asked. 'Please help me out of my confusion. Can you please stay with me for a few days? I shall serve you, great one.'

'Not for days, but I'll spend a night with you', he said with a smile."

"Darkness fell as I led him to the *kutir*. There, I prepared the high cot for him and spread my rug on the ground, so that I could sit at his feet. On asking him, if he would eat something, he said he would be happy with a banana and Ganga water. 'I hardly eat food', he said. 'This body doesn't need much'. He said that he would like to sleep for a while and not to worry as he would solve my problem in his own way. 'You sleep too,' he said, you look tired'."

"Stretching myself at his feet and wondering who he was, I quickly fell asleep. In the middle of the night, I dreamt of a deep blue pulsating light coming from inside a cave. The sound of jingling anklets came from somewhere and a sweet scent filled the air. Suddenly, someone whispered, 'wake up' and I woke up. The jingling sound of anklets continued and so did the sweet scent of incense. It came from within my *kutir*."

"I sat up and turned towards the bed. The old man was not to be seen. In his place, I saw a golden hued Buddha like figure with the eyes closed and a beauteous smile on his face. From behind him, a deep and luminescent violet blue light radiated up to the roof. Having assured myself that I was not dreaming, I prostrated before him and sat in the lotus position."

"The figure moved towards me and touched me on my head, forehead and chest. A cool breeze swept up from the bottom of my spine towards the head and warmth descended from the crown of my head and filled my heart. I was filled with pulsating deep blue light, which had its centre in the point between my eyebrows. A wave of bliss swept through my being and I discovered in a flash that I was not the heavy, conditioned body but a free being made entirely of light particles that went in and out of the heart centre in a continuous cycle, intermittently merging into and emerging from the infinite, all pervading light."

"By the time I came out of the trance, it was full day light. When I opened my eyes, there was no one to be seen, no divine figure, no *Vaishnav* sadhu; nothing except the faint scent of incense which I had smelt in the night. From that time, I have journeyed quite a bit on the path. No conflicts any more. I see clearly."

I thanked him for sharing his experience. I shared my experiences as well and at the end of ten days, I left him to go back to Chennai. We never kept in touch, but in 1996 I received a letter from Sadhu Ananda that he was going away to the Upper Himalayas near Gupt Kashi and that "we will not meet in this life again. I am sure you are doing Babaji's work. As for me, I am the eternal wanderer. *Hari Om.*"

I have not met him since but I know he is somewhere in the Himalayas, wandering in total freedom, untrammelled by the bonds of self-centred attachments.

So dear friends, if you see an old sadhu, hobbling along, perhaps begging for food, do not ignore him or avoid him. On the contrary, bow down to him, pay your respects and offer him food. Who knows which great yogi, which great Master, has come in disguise to test you, perhaps bless you and guide you.

18. Dattatreya: Lord of Avadhutas

In my previous book, I had described how I travelled to many places connected with Dattatreya as instructed by Shirdi Sai Baba. Starting from Pithapuram in Andhra Pradesh which is the birthplace of Sripada Vallabha who is said to be the second incarnation of Dattatreya, I travelled next to Narsobawadi, near Kolhapur. Narsobawadi is a beautiful little town at the confluence of the River Krishna and the River Panchganga. It derives its name from Swami Narasimha Saraswati, a monk belonging to the Dasanami order, who is considered the third manifestation of Dattatreya.

Before we proceed further, a few words about Dattatreya would be in order. Tradition has it that the ancient sage Atri and his wife Anasuya spent a long time meditating on the Singha mountain. Atri had no wish for procreation and therefore they had no children. Not only was Atri a great yogi and *rishi*, his wife Anasuya was also a powerful yogini. People flocked to take her blessings. As the story goes, the great trinity of Brahma, Vishnu and Maheshwara came to bless Anasuya, disguised as three young boys. Anasuya was taken up by the charming, divine boys and wished them to stay longer. They agreed.

Now, Anasuya developed a loving desire to become their real mother and carry them in her womb. All the three, pleased with her devotion, merged together and entered her womb. Thus Dattatreya was born and is considered as a consolidation of the Trinity. More important, Dattatreya is the patron God of all *avadhutas*, great sages and yogis, who are so immersed in the Divine, that they no longer care for the rules of social behaviour. Many of them have been known to wander around naked, oblivious of social norms.

In Maharashtra, more than in the rest of India, the name Dattatreya invokes deep devotion and is probably the most popular deity. He is shown as a wandering ascetic, sometimes with three heads representing Brahma, Vishnu and Maheshwara accompanied by a white cow and followed by a number of stray dogs.

An important philosophical work called the *Avadhuta Gita* is attributed to him. It is considered as a very early exposition of the philosophy of absolute non-dualism. It is to be noted that Dattatreya is mentioned in as ancient a text as the Atharva Veda and not a late invention as is believed by some. However, the Dattatreya movement starting from Sripada Vallabha is fairly recent (1320-1350) and was filled with such devotional fervour that today one might say that Dattatreya is by far the most popular deity in Maharashtra.

Swami Narasimha Saraswati, who was considered to be the next manifestation of Dattatreya after Sripada Vallabha, was said to have lived from 1380 to 1459. A short biographical sketch of Sri Narasimha Saraswati is as follows:

He was born to a devout Brahmin couple Amba and Madhav in Karanjanagar in the Varad region of Maharashtra. As an infant it is said that when he cried, it sounded as if he was chanting Om. The parents believed him to be a God incarnated as their son and named him Narahari – one who cuts down the sins of mankind. Till he was six years old, he did not speak and the villagers thought that he was dumb. The only word he articulated was Om.

When he was seven, it was time to perform the *Upanayana* ceremony and teach him the Gayatri mantra. The village folk wondered how a dumb child would chant the Gayatri. Somehow, his parents decided to perform the ceremony. Immediately after the Gayatri was whispered to him and he was given the sacred thread, he is said to have surprised everyone by chanting the Vedas.

He then prepared to go on a pilgrimage. However, persuaded by his mother, he agreed to stay on till she had another child. A year later, when twin boys were born to his mother, he sought permission to go to Varanasi. There he met the aged sanyasin Krishna Saraswati. On his advice, he was initiated into the ancient Dasanami order of renunciants and was given the name Sri Narasimha Saraswati. Dressed in saffron and holding the *dandi* (staff) of the Dasanamis, he set out to travel again.

He is said to have gone to Prayag and returned to his birthplace. There, he initiated his mother into the mysteries of the Divine and resumed his journey. Travelling along the banks of the Godavari and then the river Krishna, he arrived at the confluence of the Krishna and Panchganga. There was a dense forest there with a wide variety of trees including a huge number of *Audumbar* trees. A great yogi known as Ramachandra was performing austerities in the middle of the forest and assured by certain visions that a saint was to arrive, he was waiting eagerly for Sri Narasimha Saraswati.

When Sri Narasimha Saraswati walked into the forest and stood before Ramachandra Yogi, he was recognised by him and he offered Sri Narasimha Saraswati his seat. This was accepted by the great seer and he stayed under the *Audumbar* tree. In a short while, in the presence of Narasimha Saraswati, Ramachandra Yogi entered the final state of yogic development called *Mahasamadhi*, wherein the yogi voluntarily and consciously shuts down all activities of his body and goes into a trance from which he never comes back to life. This is also called *jeeva samadhi* and the tombs of such yogis, also known as *jeeva samadhis*, are worshipped in many parts of India. Ramachandra yogi's *jeeva samadhi* is located a little away from the *Audumbar* tree.

Sri Narasimha Saraswati, also called, Sri Guru is believed to have arrived at what has since been called Narsobawadi roughly in 1427 and lived there for twelve years. From there he left for Gangapur in Karnataka, where he lived for twenty years and then travelled to Srishailam in Andhra Pradesh from where he is said to have disappeared from mortal sight.

Now, the story of the *Padukas* which are worshipped by thousands of devotees every day. Roughly, six kilometres from the present Narsobawadi in Alas, lived a Deshastha Brahmin, whose name was Bahiram Bhat Jere. Both he and his wife were pious, poor and childless and led a simple life. Bahiram Bhat used to walk to nearby villages to teach and perform the ritual worship of village deities. One day whilst walking along the eastern bank of the Krishna river at the place where the *Padukas* (said to be footprints of Sri Narasimha Saraswati on a granite slab) exist now, he saw an ascetic with a shining demeanour, sitting under the *Auduambar* tree.

He crossed the river and prostrated before him. The Swami blessed him and uttered 'Narayana Narayana'. Bhat proceeded to Shiroli village and whilst going back, prostrated again. This continued for many days. One evening whilst returning home from Shiroli, Bhat went up to the Swami and prostrated as always. It was getting dark and he wanted to return home quickly. The Swami gestured to him to sit down. After a while, he prostrated again and stood up. The Swami told him that it was dark and therefore he should perform his evening religious rituals right there. The Swami assured Bhat that everything would be fine and that he need not worry about his wife. "Stay for the night," he said, "go tomorrow."

The next morning, the Brahmin was advised to go home and speak with his wife and shift his residence along with his wife permanently to the *Audumbar* forest. The Swami told him that the foot prints of Dattatreya would appear spontaneously on a stone slab, where he had himself sat and meditated for many years. The Brahmin and his wife should stay there and perform daily worship of the *Padukas*. Even though the Brahmin was sixty years old, the Swami predicted that his wife would give birth to four sons and thus the family would continue to take care of the *Padukas*.

Bahiram Bhat and his wife moved to the *Audumbar* forest and began worshipping the *Padukas* which had appeared as predicted. After making sure that the worship would continue, Sri Narasimha Saraswati went away to Gangapur in Karnataka and lived there for twenty years before disappearing into the *Kadali vana* (forest) near the temple of Srishailam in Andhra Pradesh. The priests in charge of the worship of the *Padukas* today claim to be the descendants of Bahiram Bhat. If you remember, in my autobiography, I had related the incident of Sai Baba of Shirdi giving me money and instructing me to go to all the places associated with the Dattatreya traditions. One of the places I visited then was Narsobawadi.

Getting off the bus I found myself a small room to stay. It was evening. After a bath, I went to the temple where the *Datta Padukas* are kept. One of the priests whose first name I don't remember, but whose last name was Bhat, took kindly to me and showed me all the places explaining everything in detail. After thanking him, I took leave of him and sat on the steps of the ghat for a long time. Then I went to the *samadhi* of Ramachandra Yogi. I loved that place, the solitude and a strange and blissful silence. I must have meditated there for over two hours. When I opened my eyes, it was dark all around. I decided to go back to my room and was taking out my flashlight from my kurta pocket, when a sweet fragrance filled the air.

A self-illumined, dazzling figure of a young saffron clad sanyasin stepped on to the verandah. As I looked at his face, I knew that this was indeed Sri Narasimha Saraswati. How fortunate, I said to myself. I prostrated at his feet. Blessing me by laying both his hands on my head, he said in a sweet voice, speaking in clear Hindi.

"Sai sent you here to see me. Dattatreya is the essence of all saints. Many births ago when I was at Girnar, you came to me. You were then a wandering monk determined to reach *moksha*. We spent three hours discussing your *sadhana* and past. You had a burning desire to go to the Himalayas and meet the great being called Nitya Nath, also called Sri Guru Babaji. You also mentioned that you longed to be his disciple."

"I told you that it will not be possible in that birth but you will drown in the Narmada during the floods the next year and be born after that in the Himalayas in an orthodox family whose members have been disciples of Babaji for three generations. You would thus become his disciple and fulfil your desire."

"I then initiated you into the Datta mantra – *Digambara Digambara Sripada Vallabha Digambara*."

"Do you remember it?"

"Yes Swami, I remember the mantra," I said.

"Good. So the floods came and you drowned and were born in a Garwali Brahmin family in Pandukeshwar near Badrinath. Babaji picked you up while still young and you progressed quite well. You had to however leave him and you know why."

"After many years you were born in Trivandrum, the abode of Sri Padmanabha Swami. Babaji's disciple Maheshwarnath was sent to pick you up. You know the rest of the story. Stay here for two days before you proceed to Pithapuram in Andhra Pradesh, where I manifested as Sripada Vallabha. While you are here, chant the Dattatreya mantra as many times as you can. I am going now."

As mysteriously as he had appeared, he disappeared. I walked back to my room and fell asleep instantly, fatigued by the long bus journey. I spent two days at Narsobawadi and then proceeded to Pithapuram.

19. Meeting the Buddha

I was born in a community which was considered the lowest of the low by the upper castes. I was one of those who took care of the dead bodies irrespective of their caste and burn them reducing them to ashes. The high or the low, ultimately, all turn into ashes. I was named Mooka, which also meant dumb, because until the age of five, I never spoke.

I worked in the famous Manikarnika burning ghats on the banks of the mighty river Ganga, in the ancient city of Varanasi or Benaras. Everyday hundreds of dead bodies came my way. We, the burners of the dead, were considered polluted and were outcastes. We had no access to most religious places or scriptures and naturally the only thing that gave us solace was locally made alcohol. It made us forget our humiliation and erase, even though temporarily, the memories of dealing with dead bodies day in and day out. We led a miserable existence.

However, from childhood, I had this strange desire, unusual amongst us, to hide and listen carefully to what was being said when religious discourses and philosophical debates took place, which of course took place on a daily basis in this ancient city. Gradually, by the age of thirty five, I had realised that this world which we live in had nothing much to offer. I saw how the high and mighty fell to death and was burnt to ashes. There were brief moments of joy but we were surrounded mostly by sorrow.

My wife died whilst still young and after one year, my daughter who was like a tender, dark lotus drowned in the Ganga. Life was not worth living. My only solace came from the alcohol I drank, which made me forget this harsh world. I was contemplating suicide and ending this misery once for all, but then in many religious discourses, I had heard that when one dies one comes back again to this world. 'Who knows,' I said to myself, 'these holy men must be spinning tales, but what if they are speaking the truth. Come back again into this misery! Perhaps, there is some other way to end this altogether.'

I could not summon the courage to go near any great scholar or priest and ask for help. I knew they would just dismiss me straight away even if I did – burner of dead bodies, drunk, outcaste that I was.

Then, one day an old monk wearing white robes, like those worn by the *Niganthas*, came to the Manikarnika ghat. I spotted him and wondered who he was. When he walked away, I followed him. Without turning back, he walked up to an old *peepal* tree and sat down. He saw me standing at a distance, looking at him longingly.

"Come here," he said and gestured with his right hand. I went towards him and stood at a safe distance.

"Sit down," he said.

"I am a burner of dead…," I started saying.

"I know. Come sit down," he said. I sat down.

"Tell me about yourself," he said.

I told him my story. He listened with his eyes sometimes open, sometimes closed. When I finished he said, "Now that you have emptied all that you carried inside you by speaking to me, do you feel better?" His was a kind voice.

"Yes O Great One," I said. "I feel light and happy. I had no one to talk to about all this. Do you have any instructions for me so that I may finally find lasting peace? Shall I follow you or am I disqualified because I am an untouchable?"

"I am not your teacher," he said, "but I will help you, if you follow my instructions."

"I promise."

"From today stop your work of burning dead bodies. Stop drinking alcohol. After a week, make a small thatched hut under the shade of the large *peepal* tree that stands not far from the rickety bridge that people use to cross the Varuna river. Wear only a *kaupin*, and beg for food from the Jain settlement which is a mile away. Eat only once a day. Don't kill any animal for food. Keep a clay pot filled with water from the river and a clay cup to drink water with. Have a bath in the river every day early in the morning and chant the holy OM at least for an hour with your eyes closed.'

"Continue for a month or two. One day, the great *Arhant* Gautama, who has attained enlightenment, will appear before you. He will walk on the pilgrim's path that leads to Saranganath's temple, besides which stands the deer park. He will be alone and walking towards the bridge. You will recognise him by the peace on his face and majesty of his gait. Wash his feet with water. Give him water to drink and seat him under the shade of the *peepal* tree and prostrate before him." Saying this, he got up and walked away.

The next day, I left home and followed his instructions to the dot. I built myself a small thatched hut under the *peepal* tree and ate what came by begging. I acquired an old clay pot, cleaned it well and filled it everyday with clean water from the river. I also had a new clay cup, which I never used. I was waiting for him. Meanwhile, I meditated everyday by chanting the sacred OM and watching the golden sun rising. I felt relaxed and less agitated.

Almost two months had passed when I saw what I was waiting for. On a scorching hot midday, a monk in a faded brown cloth wrapped around his body came walking barefoot on the bank of the river from the direction of Varanasi. The royal gait, majestic and leisurely, was unmistakeable.

My heart missed a beat. I ran out of my shed and stood looking at him as he approached the *peepal* tree. Now I could see the once fair but now tanned face, with beautiful features. What extraordinary features! The firmness of a *Kshatriya* and yet so delicate, almost feminine. His curly hair was tied up in a knot on the top of his head and he had very little facial hair. I ran forward and prostrated full length at his travel worn feet.

Gently, he touched my shoulders and bade me stand up saying, 'enough, enough stand up'.

Then he looked into my eyes and smiled. Oh! What a compassionate smile. I felt that I belonged to him like a child belongs to his mother. I stood looking at him speechless, my whole being filled with joy. I don't know how long I stood before I remembered what I had planned to do.

"O venerable one," I said, "I have a great desire to wash your feet and offer you some fresh water to drink. Please be kind enough to allow me to do so."

136

"So be it," said the Enlightened One.

I led him to a stone slab I had placed near the *peepal* tree and washed his feet with the water from the mud pot. I then sprinkled the water on my head and sipped a little. Drying his feet with the corner of my robe, I took him to my thatched hut and requested him to sit down. I gave him water to drink from the mud cup I had kept for him and standing before him feasted my eyes on his glorious presence.

With tears in my eyes, I folded my hands and said, "Oh Lord, glorious one, the enlightened one, how merciful and compassionate you are to come to the humble abode of the one who was a burner of the dead and accept the water offered by this low born. I have lost all interest in the terrible world of selfishness and sorrow. Please save me from this turbulent ocean of worldy existence. A venerable *Nigantha*, may he be blessed, instructed me to prostrate before you and seek help. Please help a helpless man."

"Blessed soul," said the Buddha in a powerful yet soothing voice. "Have no fear, you have now set your mind on the path. There is no low born or high born on this path. One pointedness to reach the goal is all that you need. Cross the Varuna and come to Sarnath tomorrow. In the deer park, not far from the Saranganatha temple, I shall speak the Noble Truth and turn the wheel of Dharma. Sit amongst the listeners and imbibe what I say."

"I am not your personal guru. He waits for you in the Dronagiri mountains in the Himalayas. After many births in this world and the hidden realms, you will be born in the Himalayas near Badrinath in a family of yogis and will become his disciple, but you will have to be reborn as a result of certain karmas."

"I am leaving now to go to Sarnath. After listening to the sermon at the deer park, your mind will become peaceful. Proceed towards Gomukh, the source of the Ganga. You will drown whilst bathing in the Bhagirathi in Gomukh and be reborn in a wealthy family to enjoy the fruits of washing my feet and slaking my thirst." He placed his hand on my head, blessed me and walked away towards the bridge that takes one to Sarnath. I watched him as he turned the corner and disappeared from view.

The next day, I went to Sarnath and sat a little away from the group of ascetics who sat before him. As he spoke of the noble path to nirvana, my mind was bathed in peace. He looked so glorious as if all the Gods had descended together and incarnated in that simple form of the Buddha.

As evening broke, I prostrated and returned to Varanasi. In a few days, I was on my way to Gomukh with a group of wandering ascetics.

20. My Attempt at Sanyas

I was twenty when this happened. Babaji had specifically forbidden me from becoming a sanyasin. I am not sure if it was my rebellious nature or the belief that he was perhaps testing me which prompted me to think that if I really took sanyas, he would actually be proud of me, considering he himself was a renunciant.

Maheshwarnath Babaji was away on one of his mysterious trips to an unknown destination, leaving me at the Mouni Baba cave at Rishikesh. On the other side of the Ganga was a beautiful and quiet bathing ghat, opposite a traditional and orthodox mutt. This mutt was indirectly affiliated to the ancient *Dasanami Sampradaya*, an order founded by the renowned Adi Sankara Bhagavatpada.

Occasionally, I went to this isolated ghat at four in the morning, to have a dip in the Ganga and meditate. A senior monk whom I do not want to name, from a traditional monastery known for its orthodoxy, used to frequent the ghat as well to bathe and perform his *japa*. I struck up an acquaintance with him, and several times after his *japa* we had long discussions about the deeper aspects of *Vedanta*. I found him to be a genuine soul, content and tranquil.

One day, it struck me that perhaps he might initiate me into sanyas and decided to broach the subject. So, one morning, when we sat down to have our customary discussion, I silently prayed to Maheshwarnath Babaji, and straight away asked the senior sanyasin, "Do you think I am fit for sanyas and if so, will you initiate me into the order of sanyasins?"

The old monk looked at my eyes for some time, as if trying to read my mind and then closed his eyes for a short moment and said, "I think you are quite fit to take sanyas, but there is one problem. I belong to an ancient and orthodox order and according to the rules, only the head abbot of the monastery, can give sanyas. He is bound by the rules, that only inmate novices of the monastery can be initiated into sanyas. This is apart from the fact that only novices belonging to certain communities are allowed to join the monastery. Therefore, your taking sanyas from the Ashrama officially, is out of the question."

"Now, since I know that you are qualified to take sanyas and since there is an ancient law that one who is himself a renunciant can initiate another into sanyas, provided the 'initiate' fulfils all the requirements, keeping the holy Ganga as a witness I shall initiate you into sanyas."

"I will not be breaking any rules as I will initiate you outside the ashram; I shall do it right here on the ghat. Day after tomorrow is a full moon day; shave your head on the previous day, bring two pieces of *gerua* cloth, a few flowers and a rupee coin, and meet me at four in the morning here."

I touched his feet and we parted for the time being. I was thrilled beyond measure and speculated what Babaji would say when he saw me with a shaven head, wearing *gerua* robes. I convinced myself, that he would be very happy to see me.

So, at the appointed day and hour, I waited with bated breath at the ghats. In a few minutes, the elderly swami walked down the steps. We stood facing each other. Looking carefully at his face, I noticed that there were tears flowing from his eyes and he spoke in a trembling voice and not in his usual calm and soothing tone.

He said, "Never do this again. You are not supposed to take any action without the permission of your Guru. Why didn't you tell me that your Guru had forbidden you to take sanyas?"

I said, "I am so sorry Maharaj, but I only thought that he was testing me."

He said, "Don't draw your own conclusions. Late last night, as I finished my meditation and was getting ready to sleep, somebody knocked at the door of my room. Surprised, I jumped up and opened the door. A tall, matted-hair yogi entered. He announced himself. He said, 'I am Maheshwarnath. Who on earth do you think you are to decide what steps this boy should take on his spiritual journey? I had forbidden him from taking sanyas for reasons which you don't know of. I appreciate your kind concern for him, but leave him alone. Since I am here, may I advise you to read the *Panchadasi* carefully? You require reading it again at this point'."

"With that he walked out of the room, after laying his blessed hand on my head. I am still trembling from the touch of the great Maheshwarnath Babaji, about whom I had heard on separate occasions from two senior monks in Uttarkashi. Never did I dream that the elusive Babaji will appear before me in flesh and blood. In a way, I am indebted to you for this experience, but please never commit this mistake of disobeying your Guru. If a great yogi like him says you are not to take sanyas, no one can change that."

I prostrated at his feet, sought his forgiveness and thanked him for still being so kind to me. I could not meet him after that incident.

Babaji returned, took one look at my shaven head and said, "It will take some time for the hair to grow back. Actually you look very nice with a shaven head, but sanyas is not for you. So no more misadventures. Tomorrow, early in the morning, we start for Uttarkashi."

That was the end of my aspiration to become a formal *gerua* clad sanyasin.

21. Conversations with Babaji – 3

M: Babaji, I have had the opportunity of studying the *Mandukya Upanishad* and I know that *Gaudapada's karika* – commentary is exhaustive, but I have been unable to fully grasp the treatise on the different states of consciousness.

Babaji: I will start with a story as a first step. King Janaka who came to be known as *Raja Rishi*, sage amongst kings, once had a dream. He dreamt that he was a beggar walking around with his begging bowl, hungry, tired and in tattered clothes. On waking up, he found himself amidst the splendours of the palace.

This set him thinking – Am I a beggar or a king? Whilst in the dream, he clearly felt that he was a beggar. The pangs of hunger and weariness no less real than the luxuries of the palace when he woke up. As he was unable to solve this puzzle, he sought the aid of the great sage Yajnavalkya, who explained to him the different states of consciousness that makes this world real, unreal or non-existent. Though this story has no direct link with the *Mandukya Upanishad*, the topic discussed is the same in both.

Now listen carefully. The different states of consciousness are *jagritaavastha* – the waking state, *swapnaavastha* – the dream state, *suptaavastha* or *sushupti* – deep, dreamless state and *turiyaavastha* – the transcendental state that lies beyond

143

the previous three states. Consciousness functions in all the three states. When one is awake, the dream state seems to be unreal, but during the dream, no reality other than the dream exists. The dream is so real that all senses function, all emotions are experienced.

The difference between the two states is that the waking state lasts longer than the dream state and is therefore more real. In the dream state, there is no awareness of the difference between the states. In deep dreamless sleep, neither of the states is perceived by the consciousness, as if consciousness itself were non-existent. In the dream state, the subtle sense organs replicate the actions of the five sense organs of the waking state. In deep sleep not only do these organs – both physical and subtle – but also the mind cease to function.

Ahamkara loosely translated as ego, individuality or the 'I' factor ceases its extrovert activites and traces its way back to the finer parts of itself called *buddhi*, the intellect, which forms the basic consciousness in a human being that feels 'I exist'. Since the *ahamkara* does not function during deep sleep, the feeling 'I exist' is not experienced.

In deep sleep, all the experiences of the waking and dream state seem to have disappeared and the consciousness enjoys peace and bliss without being impacted or affected by the external world of senses or the internal world of dreams. The paradox of this state is that, on analysing the experience, one does not know whether one was conscious or unconscious. All that can be said is that it is contentless or negative consciousness or a consciousness not aware of itself. You may, however, ask whether there is any consciousness during deep sleep which can enjoy peace and bliss? How could there be an absence of consciousness if on waking up one feels and says, 'I had a wonderful undisturbed sleep'? Undoubtedly, there is something while in deep sleep which is capable of experiencing that state of tranquility and which is able to differentiate it from the experiences of the waking and dream states.

Turiya, the fourth state, is not one of the states like the other three. It is present in all states, even in that state of pure consciousness when *ahamkara* is dropped. It is this consciousness that is called the *Atman* or spirit and is the sole witness of waking, dream and sleep states as also of the various altered states of consciousness like trance, *samadhi* etc.

In *turiya*, consciousness is in its pristine purity and has no separate identity from that all pervading Universal Consciousness, *Brahman*. Hence the rishi says, '*Ayam Atma Brahman*, my Atman is Brahman'. It is the attainment of the same consciousness which is referred to by the statement *Aham Brahmasmi*, I am *Brahma*. No one can proclaim *Aham Brahmasmi* and remain a limited human being for, where there is even an iota of *aham*, there cannot be Absolute *Brahman*.

The point to be stressed is that *turiya* is not comparable to the waking, dream and deep sleep states. In all these three states, there continues a sense of self-identity, there is a subject and an object or an experience and the experienced, even though such a distinction is not manifest or realised at the time of experiencing. In *turiya*, there is no distinction between the experience and the experienced or the subject and the object and it is that consciousness that is subject to disturbances and changes. In the other three states, the relative consciousness, specific to that state, excludes the other states. For example, in the dream state, the reality of the waking world is absent and vice-versa; the king becomes a beggar and a beggar becomes a king.

On attaining *turiya*, the experiencing individual self is subsumed under the Universal Self or *Atman*. He who has attained or merged in *turiya* can see the *Atman* in all three states when he descends to relative consciousness, for the *Atman*, never ceases to exist. The three states are mere illusions like different moving pictures seen on the same screen.

That person is the true Sanyasin or renunciant, untouched by anything whatsoever, who is ever established in the bliss of the *Brahman* irrespective of his activity or inactivity. It is only he who if fully relaxed and at peace, for he is beyond deep sleep and rests in the calmness of that which is the root of all activity. He is the sole witness to the rising and falling of the waves of creation and destrucion. For one who is established in *turiya*, the entire world of experience is like a long dream from which he has woken up. He is face to face with the Ultimate Reality beyond all dreams; in fact he is himself the Reality.

22. Mind and Other Matters

B abaji began by saying that we would discuss some more about the mind, and how the same mind that binds and conditions you can also open the channel through which flows abundant energy from the cosmic source.

He started with a story as he said that stories are the most suitable as explanatory illustrations; even small children understand them.

One day, a wizened old man in rags was literally dragging himself along the side of a busy road. He was so emaciated and weak that every step he took seemed to be a painful ordeal. All of a sudden, a car coming at full speed screeched to a halt just behind him with its horn blaring. The old man, who a second ago looked as if he would fall at any moment, leapt on the pavement to a safe distance far from the car.

How did he do that? A moment earlier, he could not have had any inkling of the imminent danger so that he could save himself. Then, what saved him? It was a split-second reflex action. The message 'jump and save your life', must have flashed into his brain and the message was transmitted instantly to his limbs. Adrenalin was released immediately and his muscles reacted.

The point to note here is that there was no intereference from the conditioned mind and the prejudiced thought process. If thought had interfered, he could not have reacted so quickly. He would instead still be thinking how can an old, weak person like him jump out of the car's way when he didn't even have the energy to walk, whilst the vehicle crushed him.

In this emergency situation, the message 'jump' came directly without being conditioned or influenced by thought. He was drawing energy directly from the cosmic source, although involuntarily.

What this man achieved involuntarily can be achieved by a yogi voluntarily. The yogi learns the technique of quelling the otherwise constant vibrations or ripples of his mind and making himself receptive to the flow of energy from the Cosmic Mind whenever he feels the need. This is the secret of the first sentence in that masterpiece of yoga, the *Patanjali Yoga Sutra*, which says '*Yoga chitta vritti nirodha*'. That is, yoga is the elimination of the *vrittis*, the disturbing waves of the *chitta*, the mind stuff. This is how the yogi gains access to the cosmic source of wisdom and energy. Not only does he develop the capacity to receive messages, but also send messages as it were to the fourth dimension to get answers.

The main centre he makes use of for this purpose is the brain, which is the seat of the mind and more specifically, the two major centres of the brain known in yogic terms as the *ajna* and *sahasrara* chakras. Note that the word used is chakra, meaning a wheel. Actually, chakra implies a whirlpool like area, a junction where the cosmic energy can be observed by a clairvoyant, whirling constantly and exhibiting myriad colours. It is through these centres that cosmic energy enters the human body.

Yogic anatomy identifies each of these existing chakras with a corresponding nerve plexus on the spinal chord of the human system called the *sushumna naadi*, the central channel. The exceptions are the upper two chakras which are intimately connected with the functioning of the two tiny ductless glands, the pituitary and the pineal glands situated in the brain. Starting from the lowest, the chakras are the *muladhara* at the base of the spine, the *swadhisthana* slightly above it, the *manipura* at the level of the navel, the *anahata* at the level of the heart, the *visuddha* in the area of the neck and the *ajna* and *sahasrara*, I mentioned earlier.

I shall now explain the secret of *Laya Yoga* or *Kundalini Yoga*.

In every human being resides the cosmic energy called the *Kundalini Shakti*, coiled three and a half times and symbolised by a serpent, at the base of the spine in the *muladhara chakra*. However, in all, except the yogi who has mastered the technique of awakening this energy, it remains inactive although potent like a coiled spring. Using a technique, which can only be learned directly from a *Guru* and not by any other means, the yogi succeeds by constant effort in awakening the *kundalini* and leading it upwards, piercing chakra after chakra, to finally reach the *sahasrara* chakra at the top.

As the *kundalini* pierces each chakra, the conduits are cleared of all impurities that have been blocking them. As the *kundalini* ascends and each chakra opens up, the yogi reaches newer and newer dimensions of power and his links with the Cosmic Energy become closer. The powers which he exhibits are called *siddhis* in yogic parlance. The perfect *siddha* is the one whose *kundalini* has opened the *sahasrara* chakra and who thereby attains the capacity to harness the very source of Cosmic Energy.

Now, I will tell you more about the *ajna* and *sahasrara* chakras. These are the most important ones that have a direct bearing on knowledge. The *ajna* chakra is situated in the forehead, just behind the point where the eyebrows meet. It is also known as *trikuta* or *bhroomadhya* and is symbolised by the third eye of Shiva who is himself the symbol of transformation and regeneration. It is when this centre is activated that the practising yogi becomes clairvoyant. He acquires the ability to use the chakra as an instrument to perceive subtle forces in dimensions beyond the world of sense perception.

Just as a drop seen under a microscope reveals it as a complex ever active system of dancing particles, the universe reveals its mysteries to the yogi who uses his special perceptive faculty of the *ajna* chakra. He thus comes to possess knowledge that the ordinary man does not have access to. The *ajna* chakra is the transmitting station from which the yogi can send messages in the form of thought waves to other humans or to highly evolved beings.

The *sahasrara* chakra is the highest centre. When the *kundalini* reaches this centre and activates it, the yogi is able to link directly to the essence of the universe. This is called *samadhi*. This accounts for the immense wisdom which great yogis, who may be considered illiterate, display when they have attained *samadhi*. The pineal gland, which was once considered a vestige organ without any known function, has a major part to play in activating the *ajna*

and *sahasrara* chakras. I shall teach you later how to harness these energies. The main point to remember is that the
practice of *kundalini yoga* is linked to the sublimation of
sexual energies but not by repression, suppression or any
forcible method.

(*Note to readers*: The practical techniques cannot be
given in print or by any other method without the
direct personal mediation of the teacher. They have
to be learnt from a personsal adept. I was warned by
Babaji that revealing the techniques through books
or some other secondary methods would be dange-
rous to the novice. In his words, "Bear in mind that
the yogi is playing with forces more powerful than
electricity or even atomic energy; a wrong move can
physically or mentally wreck the student.")

M: In the practical exercises you taught me relating to
kundalini yoga, there is a lot of visualisation; one has to
imagine so many things. What bothers me is the thought
that by allowing my imagination to grow, wouldn't I be
cut off from reality and live in a perpetual dream world? Is
imagination a sign of mental progress or decadence? Please
enlighten me.

Babaji: Thought is the mother of all action. So also is imagination or visualisation, the key to all achievement. Imagination is not the sign of a diseased mind. On the contrary, it
is the sign of a healthy and rich mind. Only when it is not
controlled or is allowed to run riot, does it become harmful.

Controlled and deliberate imagination is in fact the sign of a genius. Great scientists, artists, indeed humans in all fields of endeavour, have always had a rich imagination. The very beginning of any creative venture is imagination.

The artist, for instance, visualises everything in detail before he puts it on canvas. Ask a successful and wealthy man and he will tell you how he, in his days of poverty, had visualised in great detail, the house he would live in, the car he would drive, the clothes he would wear, the money he would handle, once he came by his riches. By keeping these images constantly in his mind and working hard on the ideas, he slowly transforms his dreams into reality. This is regarding the world of senses.

In the subtle world, the results are instantaneous – one does not have to wait for long. Every passing thought leaves its impression on the invisible world of fine matter that surrounds us. But when one particular image is deliberately contemplated upon, and that too in full detail – colour, form, shape and so on, a strong image is actually created in the subtle world. Great yogis create positive thought forms and direct them towards humans who are in need of them. Only the yogi who has reached the highest level is able, by a mere thought, to transform his vision into physical reality. Such persons are rare and should not be confused with magicians who perform sleight of hand tricks. However, such rare, divine persons, as a rule, never demonstrate their powers except under specific conditions.

So develop the habit of visualising good and beautiful objects – for instance, a full grown rose or the word *Aum* in Devanagari script in electric blue or gold – every morning in your mind's eye and spread happiness and good will mentally to the whole world as you wake up.

Visualise your desires in complete detail and you are sure to attain them, but never visualise harm to others, for that will arrest your own spiritual development and pull you down the ladder of spiritual evolution. You can imagine yourself to a state of happiness or unhappinesss, it is your choice.

M: I have had my doubts cleared about imagination. However, I am puzzled by the yogic statement, 'the meditator and the object of meditation become one in deep meditation.' If I contemplate a tree, how can I become one with the tree?

Babaji: You have misunderstood the meaning of the sentence, as so many others have. There are three stages in meditation. In the first stage, *dharana*, one concentrates on a particular object. When the smooth flow of concentration continues uninterrupted for a long time, one is in *dhyana*. The culmination of *dhyana* is *samadhi*, in which state the meditator forgets himself and the only idea that exists in his mind is that of the object that he meditates upon. Then, nothing but the object exists for the time being. In that state, the object is peeled layer by layer and the yogi derives knowledge of the object in all its aspects.

Those who follow the path of discrimination, the *jnana yogi*, however interpret it in a slightly different manner. According to them, the 'experience and the experienced are one'. To make it clearer, let me ask you a few questions. When you say that you are meditating on, for instance, *Aum*, what happens?

M: I close my eyes and imagine a gold coloured *Aum* shining in my heart.

Babaji: Who imagines the *Aum*?

M: I, my mind.

Babaji: When you say I, doesn't that mean the whole collection of thoughts that is your mind, your past experiences, your emotions, your reactions etc?

M: Yes, that's true.

Babaji: Isn't the *Aum* that is visualised another form of thought, also a part of your mind?

M: Yes.

Babaji: So, isn't the differentiation between the collection of thoughts you called 'I' and the *Aum*, that is visualised, an artificial partition raised by thought itself? Isn't the experience and the experienced both thought – the mind itself? Then, where is the difference between the experience and the experienced? They are the same entity, the mind, a collection of thoughts.

M: I understand what you mean, Babaji. When the artificial barrier disappears, all that remains is the field in which so many thoughts appear and disappear. As I watch the appearing and disappearing of thoughts perfectly aware that I, the watcher, am only a part of that unceasing wave of thoughts, my mind begins to rest.

* * * * *

At this point, without any conscious attempt, I entered into a meditative state, the duration of which I cannot remember. The incessant thought waves must have lost their identity and merged into the source from which they were created, for when I came out of that state, I felt an inexpressible and inordinate bliss of silence and peace. Babaji must have watched me and understood my state, for his next words were, "Bless you. Continue to enjoy the ocean of peace with the full awareness that you too are only part of the field of thoughts called mind and you will lose your finite identity. What will be left over is the infinite, thoughtless reality – the Supreme Peace."

* * * * *

M: Babaji, is *pranayama* considered a great aid in meditation? How does it help a yogi?

Babaji: You have touched the crux of an important misconception. Associating *pranayama* only with meditation and yogic practices is a common error. I must make it clear that *pranayama* is a true science and in its proper form, it should be taken up by all for their benefit. It helps them as much as it does the yogi.

Before I give you some practical hints, which many students of yoga may not have come across, let me tell you that many of the secrets of *pranayama* have applications in material welfare as well. If you wonder how a practice that yields material benefits can be useful for spiritual progress, you should know that *Vedic* teachings are not, as generally supposed, concerned only with spiritual salvation, liberation or *moksha*. They deal as much with *dharma*, the pursuit of righteousness; *artha*, the acquisition of wealth; and *kama*, desire or pleasure. They deal with the how and why of good conduct whether one is a householder or a sanyasin, the business of living that includes trade and commerce or any activity contributing to material welfare and the legitimate satisfaction of one's desires.

That is why according to *vedic* tradition, the entire life span of a person is divided into four stages called *ashramas*.

The first stage is *brahmacharyashrama* when a person apprentices himself to one or more teachers to learn all that will equip him for the next stage, *grihasthashrama*. In this stage, he is fully engaged in the world – marriage, children, earning a livelihood etc. Once the duties of the world are fulfilled and the children are grown up and can fend for themselves, the person and his wife together seek places of solitude like a forest to contemplate the mysteries of a higher life, a spiritual life. This is called *vanaprasthashrama*.

The last stage is *sanyasashrama*. In this, a person who has contemplated on the world and the subtle spheres, and has more than an intellectual grasp of the insubstantiality of the world, has decided to renounce it for a life that leads him to the Ultimate Reality whilst sustaining his body as a mendicant. Sanyasa, mind you, is adopted voluntarily. One is not bound by any law or compulsion to this *ashrama*. In fact, there have been great spiritual luminaries who remained householders till the very end of their earthly existence. If a person, by virtue of his great detachment and dispassion, took to sanyasa, he was however, given a special place in society and regarded as divine. There have been such great souls in our recent memory.

Most people have to pass through all these stages. It is the rare exceptions who, having worked out all their *karmas*, drop the two intermediate stages and leap straight from *brahmacharya* to sanyasa.

The real science of *pranayama* does not mean the forcible control or retention of breath. It means the study of applying the laws under which the *prana* or the life force operates in the human body and affects it physically, mentally and spiritually. If you bear in mind that *prana* is not just the air that is breathed in and breathed out but is the magnetic cosmic energy sustaining the body, then you will realise that its proper utilisation is of great importance, spiritually and temporally.

In other words, it is not meant only for those interested in spiritual salvation. Those who are caught up in the day-to-day business of life too can derive material benefits of *pranayama*. Perhaps, after attaining their material well being and still continuing with the practice, they may gradually enter the field of spiritual endeavour by virtue of the proper control of *prana*.

The *prana* can be controlled by one who knows the theory and practical techniques of *pranayama*. When we go to sleep, keeping our heads towards south and feet towards north ensures a tension-free, restful sleep. In this position, the direction of the body is in accordance with the direction of the earth, thereby maintaining a harmonious balance with the earth's magnetic field.

I shall now tell you about the channels through which the *prana* flows. According to yogic science, especially *Sivasamhita*, the entire nervous system is a delicately interwoven network of 72,000 nerves or *nadis*. Of these, only three are considered as important channels of energy from a practical yogic point of view. They are the *sushumna*, the *ida* and the *pingala*. The *sushumna* is the organ through which energy is conducted.

The *ida* and the *pingala* coordinate and control all the voluntary and involuntary functions of the human body, which an adept can at will. The *sushumna*, which is linked to the spinal chord, is the central channel and the *ida* and the *pingala* are situated on either side of it. The *ida*, which is on the left of the *sushumna*, starts from the left nostril and the *pingala*, on the right of the *sushumna* from the right nostril. Both terminate at the coccyx or *muladhara*.

Here is an important thing to remember – breath does not flow through both nostrils at all times in any human being. The flow of breath alternates between the two nostrils every ninety minutes. The yogis have understood the importance of the shifting cycles in influencing the various states of the mind. You must have heard of the functions of the two hemispheres of the brain, you may be aware that the right hemisphere which controls the left side of the body, influences visual imagination, music appreciation, intuitive perception etc. The left hemisphere, which controls the right side of the body, is the seat of such capabilities as language, logic, analytical thought, sense of rhythm etc. By constant practice of *pranayama*, a yogi becomes an adept at activating at will either of the hemispheres.

M: Could you please explain the proper place of faith in religious pursuits.

Babaji: Faith is nothing to laugh at. The entire world, including that of science, depends on faith. At school, you study all about the universe in your science books. Since you are not in a position to explore what has been stated, for instance, that there are nine planets in our solar system that revolve around the sun, you accept it on faith. Of course, as you grow, you might get an opportunity to find out for yourself whether what you have accepted on faith is true or not. Until then, you pin your faith on the sincerity of the scientist who stated it and the textbook that you read.

Would it not be foolish to deny the existence of the nine planets straight away because you haven't seen or you can't see them? Of course, the really intelligent student wouldn't either accept of deny it straightaway; he would accept on faith until he finds the means to enquire into it first hand.

This is the kind of faith that is required of the earnest religious seeker. He has to merely suspend judgement about the truths the sages have uttered, after experiencing what is beyond the ordinary man's capacity to explore. Meanwhile, he should try to develop in himself the faculties that lie outside our sensory organs and conditioned thought. Once he has reached the same state as a sage who proclaimed a particular thought, he is at liberty to accept or discard it. One who denies a statement without enquiry builds a mental obstruction that blocks all knowledge. How can one seek something which one has denied off-hand?

Vedanta therefore encourages healthy discussion and many of the Upanishads are in the form of discussions between and among various rishis, teachers and their disciples. These discussions are serious because they are sincere joint efforts to arrive at the solution to a specific problem and not mere indulgence in futile sophistry, parading one's knowledge or the pastime of an idle hour. They are the very essence of Vedantic study and serve to sharpen the intellect of the seeker to help him deal with the subjects of a subtle nature.

You should also note that the word faith is *shraddha* in Sanskrit and is translated into English as faith. Faith is not an accurate translation of *shraddha*. *Shraddha* means one pointed attention, the sacred care given to one's endeavour. When a person has unquestioned faith in his own capacity for achieving his goal, whether spiritual or temporal, he is not disturbed by negative thoughts that weaken the will and discourage the spirit. Not disturbed by any demoralising thought, the person who has faith persists in his efforts till the very end and attains what he sets out to do.

That is why it is said that faith can move mountains. That kind of faith does not contradict reason but complements it. Have faith in your essential divinity son, and you will achieve what looks impossible. Test your faith certainly by gathering first hand information and experience, but these moods of doubt and scepticism will gradually vanish. A person becomes doubtless only after he has attained *turiya*.

There is a limit to everything including the dose of teaching that can be given at a time. Too much would be wasted since your mind would not be able to grasp it, too little would give you the idea that this is all there is to knowledge and therefore you are all-knowing. Your eagerness to learn more shows that you realise your shortcomings. It is a good sign, the sign of a sincere student.

Before we finish this session, I will tell you a story that will be of great use to all sincere seekers; the story of Ananda, the great disciple of Buddha. In spite of his devotion to his master, he once became extremely agitated and perplexed by what seemed to him an unsolvable problem. Doubts assailed him, so much so that he came to question the very teachings of Buddha. Conflicting emotions overwhelmed him and as an escape from his anguish and restlessness, he began to pace the rough ground with such intensity that his feet began to bleed. Yet the solution remained elusive.

The Buddha had been watching him for some time. Moved by the turmoil of his beloved disciple, the Buddha beckoned to him. "Ananda," he said looking kindly at him, "bring your veena and play me a lovely tune. Relax now. We will tackle your problem later."

Ananda was a highly accomplished musician. He brought out his veena and was on the verge of playing, when his master interrupted. "Slacken the strings," he said. Ananda was perplexed at this strange command but obeyed. "Now play," the Buddha said.

"How can I when the strings are slack?" asked Ananda. "All right," said the Buddha, "tighten the strings." When they became taut enough to play and he was ready, the Buddha said, "Tighten them more." "The strings are sure to snap, my Lord." said Ananda.

The great teacher smiled, "Ananda, I have no need to listen to the music. Whenever I have the need, I can listen to the music of the spheres. I took you through these motions only to bring home a point. Just as the strings of a veena should be tightened only to an optimum level for tuneful music, so should the mind be stretched to its right limit for effective performance, no more, no less.

A lazy mind like the slackened strings that produce only dull notes, can have only hazy and sluggish thoughts. Similarly, a mind stretched beyond its capacity is tensed and incapable of clear thinking. In such a mind, thoughts rush in so fast that there cannot be coherence. Leave alone coherence, such a mind is likely to collapse under the strain and even lead to insanity. The key to clear thinking and problem solving is therefore an alert but relaxed mind. Concentration is not tension. On the contrary, it is possible only when the mind is relaxed but attentive."

M: In the case of a great soul like Ananda, such a state of mind could have occurred only rarely. But what about ordinary people like me who are prone to frequent doubts – what shall I do when doubts assail me?

Babaji: This is not a phenomenon peculiar to you. Every sincere aspirant passes through these dark moods; they are the tools that Nature's negative forces use to test the sincerity of the aspirant. Great saints have had these moods. Don't worry, these moods pass. In spiritual terms, this state is called the 'dark night of the soul'.

When such a mood comes, meditate calmly, chant the sacred *Aum* or just relax by listening to melodius music. Don't take any serious decisions. Wait till your mind becomes free of tension. A person who knows the secret of *pranayama* can get over this condition easily.

After the 'dark night of the soul', a new day dawns and you will be able to think clearly. Once your mind attains the capacity to experience the spiritual bliss personally and you begin to depend less on what others have taught you and what you have read and when practical experiences replace theoretical knowledge, all your doubts will vanish and your progress on the spiritual path will accelerate.

Aum Tat Sat.

23. The compassion of Sri Ramakrishna

Just before I was born a boy in a Muslim family in Kerala, I was born a courtesan's daughter in Sonagatchi, the red light district of Calcutta. My mother was an upper-class courtesan and catered only to the elite babus. Naturally, I was trained in the same profession and being talented in dance and music and the art of making love, I was a much sought after young woman. My name was Sashikala.

One of my clients, who came from a respectable family and whose name for obvious reasons I shall not reveal, one day said to me in a drunken state, "Shoshi, people like you who the public considers sinners, and without whose company, I would have committed suicide long ago, are now blessed. There lives a saint in the Kalibari of Rani Rasmoni who is so compassionate; he blesses even the likes of you and me."

"Girish Ghose, the famous dramatist of Star Theatre, who needs no introduction and who drinks, fornicates and calls himself, 'the king of sinners' said to me the other day with tears in his eyes, "Young man, even a fellow like me now has a saviour. Thakur has been born to redeem our sins. I went to him fully drunk one night and abused him. He seated me on his lap and fed me *sandesh* with such love."

"I heard he will be visiting the Star Theatre tomorrow to watch Girish dada's play Chaitanya Leela. Would you like to see him there? I am planning to go but if you go and see me around please do not drop even the slightest hint that we are acquainted."

I told him that I was anyway not inclined to go just to see a so-called saint because I did not believe in holymen and their holier-than-thou attitude. With that, the conversation ended.

The next evening, a strange force prompted me to go to the theatre. When I arrived at the theatre, it was very late and the show was over. The saint was about to depart. Girish Chandra Ghosh was prostrating full length at his feet, which surprised me for he was an alcoholic and womaniser apart from being a famous dramatist. What really attracted me was the simple and tender expression of love that emanated from the eyes of the saintly man; a face that gleamed with the light of an inner joy, which he seemed to be constantly enjoying.

He wore a white dhoti with a red border, a white kurta and a black coat over it. On his feet he wore brown polished slip on shoes. His lips were stained red with *paan* and contrasted with his extremely fair face. No outward sign of holiness, no beads, no saffron robe, no longer beard and no airs about him. He was surrounded by famous actors, some babus and an extraordinarily handsome young man who I later learnt was Narendra Nath Dutta, the saint's closest disciple. I fell in love with both of them instantly.

Looking around, the saint whom everybody seemed to call Thakur saw me standing at a distance. He gestured to me to come forward. Reluctantly, I moved towards him. The crowd made way. Before I knew it, my head was at his feet. "No, no!" he exclaimed, "get up little mother." I stood up. His eyes met mine. He placed his hands on my head and blessed me saying, "May the mother who lives in your heart awaken." A strange and ecstatic energy filled my heart. Tears fell from my eyes. I wept my heart out. Narendra Dutta who stood on my right said almost in a whisper, "Control yourself. You are fortunate." I turned and looked at those calm eyes of the young disciple. I felt like giving him a hug and then felt ashamed of my earthly thoughts.

Thakur, whilst getting into the carriage, turned around and said, "Come to Dakshineshwar, mother." I stood rooted to the spot as the carriage gathered speed and disappeared. Narendra Dutta had also gone with his master.

*****

One Friday morning, after two weeks of hesitation, I just decided to go to Dakshineshwar. Hiring a horse carriage (buggy) from Kolkata and then boarding a boat, I crossed the Hooghly river and entered Dakshineshwar from the ghat.

"Go straight towards the Ma Kali temple," said the Muslim boatman, "See? Right there," he pointed.

I could see the pinnacle of a temple at a distance. I walked towards it and entered the temple courtyard. Being Friday, a day special to the Goddess, there was a big rush. This was the first time, I was here. I was not much of a temple goer and was myself surprised at my happiness, the reason for which I could not lay my finger on.

Perhaps it was the anticipation of meeting Thakur, the *Paramahamsa*, with whom I seemed to have fallen in love. It took nearly half an hour to get close to the sanctum sanctorum. The mother goddess Kali looked so sweet even in her most destructive manifestation. I forgot the world as I stood looking at her. Someone said, "Hey move, make way for others, move, move."

I saluted the deity and came out of the sanctum. In the courtyard, near the gate, I asked someone, "Do you know where the *Paramahamsa* lives?"

"*Paramahamsa*? Ah! The mad priest," he said and studied me closely. "I know you," he said, "go out of the gate and turn left. People say he associates with prostitutes, when he is not with his boys. Go go, right person for you."

"Go to hell!" I said to him wishing that mother Kali would behead him and walked away. His directions were however right. I found myself on the verandah of a small room filled with a dozen people or so. As I stood at the door and looked inside, I saw the blessed Thakur, sitting on a cot, one leg folded, the other touching the ground. Near him on the floor, amongst other youngsters, sat Narendra Dutta of the beautiful eyes with tabla drums in front of him. The Master glanced at me. Narendra said, "The young woman who you blessed at the theatre has come."

"I know," said Thakur, "it's the opium. Have it once and you are hooked forever. There is nothing more intoxicating than God-consciousness." Every one laughed. I was in a daze. It was as if a dream had been fulfilled. I laughed loudly. Somebody came near me and said rudely, "Move out of my way. Don't go inside. This is a sacred place. If you want to sit, sit on the side of the verandah."

I moved away and sat near the steps. I couldn't see inside but could hear what was going on. One of my infrequent clients, a very rich babu, who was also sitting at the other end of the verandah saw me and averted his eyes. He pretended not to recognise me for a while and then with a furtive expression, got up and walked away.

A beautiful song on the Mother Shyama, sung in a mellifluous voice to the accompaniment of the tabla, came wafting from the room. Part of the song said, "So Ma Shyama has entered me. I am so drunk with ecstasy that I am no more and Shyama above sits here." A visitor sitting near me said, "That's Noren singing for his master." The song stopped and a blissful silence entered my heart.

After a while Thakur's unmistakable voice with a slight stammer and childlike was heard saying, "Look here, all that might be true but I like to think of myself as separate. She is the sugar and I am the ant that sucks and enjoys it."

Narendra's voice was heard saying, "For me it's all one, the Supreme Brahman, one without a second, the Blissful One."

"Ma go," said Thakur in a half cloaked voice and the next thing I saw was that he was coming out of the room, tottering like a drunk and with Naren supporting him. I looked up from the steps and a strange thing happened. Thakur's form had vanished and in his place I saw the mother Shyama, so beautiful, dark with red lips and crystal white teeth walking towards me.

Shyama touched my chin and kept saying "Ah! I am inside you too girl." I was in deep ecstasy and my body shook as I sobbed uncontrollably. I fell at his feet and surrendered my life to him. I don't know how long I was in that state. When I woke up, I was lying in a strange little room under the staircase. My head was on a woman's lap. She was stroking my hair.

"How are you feeling child?" said a kind voice that came from the kindest face I have ever seen in my life. Later, I came to know that she was Mother Sharada Devi, the wife of Thakur. Holding her hand, I sobbed again.

"It's all right child," she consoled me. "Today, Thakur blessed you. You are a fortunate girl. Go wash your face, darling."

After I washed my face and came back, she combed my hair and fixed a hibiscus flower. "From the Mother's offerings," she said. "Thakur has gone to Calcutta with Naren and others. Now before you go, I need to tell you something confidential. Thakur told Naren and he told me. Listen carefully. You will not come back here again. This is your first and last visit. Your life on this earth, this time will soon come to an end."

"Thakur said to tell you that from many past births, you have been a disciple of the great *Chiranjeevi* Himalayan yogi Bawaji. Due to certain actions of yours in the past and to learn certain lessons, you have come in this form in this birth. In the next birth, the Himalayan Bawaji will re-establish contact with you."

"At the precise time when you leave this body, child, Thakur will be there to bless you. Go home now, should I ask someone to accompany you?"

"No mother," I said and prostrated at her feet. I was composed and my heart was at peace as I bid farewell.

*****

When I reached home, my mother said, "Your face is glowing and so peaceful. Did you meet Thakur and did you have darshan of Kali Ma?"

I only said to her, "Yes Ma, I did. It is so peaceful there."

I stopped seeing clients although that meant that I had no income. My mother protested, but I stood firm. "I'll find some other job," I said, "Perhaps Girish Babu will give me a role in his next production."

Three weeks after my visit to Dakshineshwar, one Friday evening, my mother and I were sitting in the verandah of our little house. My mother was oiling and combing my hair. All of a sudden, I felt a piercing pain in my chest and leaned my head on my mother's lap.

"Soshi, Soshi," my mother kept saying, "What happened? Shall I send somebody to call the doctor? Soshi...."

The pain ceased as suddenly as it had started. It was replaced by a feeling of deep tranquility. The world around me faded. I could no longer hear my mother's voice. A lovely fragrance of jasmine was in the air.

Then I saw Mother Kali, swirling beautifully and standing in front of me. She bent and kissed me on my forehead and when she straightened up, she was transformed into my beloved Thakur. "I have come to take you," said Thakur, "Come, my child. Look to your left. There stands the Himalayan sage Babaji, your Guru in previous births."

To his right, stood a most beautiful Being, fair with long brown hair and wearing just a short white loin cloth. In an instant I recognised him and shouted with joy, "Babaji!"

"You have one more life to go before you get back to me," said Babaji. I will send my close disciple Maheswar to establish contact with you. You will be born as a boy in a Muslim family."

"Now we have come to take you across the barrier that separates this life and the next. After your soul rests in bliss, preparations will be made to decide the next birth. Om Shanti!"

By now, I could see that I had separated from the body. My mother was holding the body and crying. Both Thakurji and Babaji held my hands. We floated for a while and then, I felt I was passing into a deep and blissful slumber. Everything vanished into *Akasha*[1].

---

1   According to the ancient Sankhya philosophy, *Akasha* is the primordial and undifferentiated state of *prakriti* – nature – from which the diverse forms emerge and ultimately merge back into. Out of the subtlest *Akasha* arise *Vayu, Agni, Apas* and *Prithvi*, Prithvi being the grossest. During *pralaya* or dissolution of the cosmos, they merge into Akasha.

   The yogi, therefore, raises his consciousness from the gross *Prithvi* through *Apas, Agni* and *Vayu* and beyond that to its origin which is The Supreme Consciousness called *Purusha* in Sankhya as well as in Yoga. This state is known as *Kaivalya*.

24. Yoga: Philosophy and Practice

This is one of the conversations I had with Babaji on the banks of the Ganga at Arundhati Cave.

M: Babaji, how ancient are the teachings of Yoga?

Babaji: The yogic teachings are so ancient that it is difficult to trace their origins. The oldest Upanishads contain portions dealing with yogic science and mention them as ancient teachings. They are part of the knowledge that has come to us from a pre-historic glorious civilization now extinct. Just before that civilization perished due to a massive natural catastrophe, these wise men saved the teachings referring to the yogic sciences, in safe geographical locations. From there, they were disseminated bit by bit according to the receiving capacity of the aspirants.

The earliest compiler of this science was Patanjali, who wrote the *Yoga Sutra*, aphorisms on yoga and is himself considered a mystical half human, half snake figure, the great teacher from Naga Loka. *Yajnavalkya Samhita* or the yogic teachings of the great Upanishadic sage, Yajnavalkya is also an important text.

Over time, when the teachings of certain sects became popular and the false idea that one is essentially pure consciousness, and that this can be simply grasped through intellectual reasoning and mere repetition of *Aham Brahm-asmi* – I am the Brahman, was propagated, yoga the actual practice of the step by step methods of altering the thought process to bring about the state of mind required to experience the Brahman or the pure infinite consciousness, fell into disuse and would have been lost but for the teachings of the *Bhagavad Gita* and later on the teachings of the Nath *Sampradaya* (tradition).

The Naths, especially Gorakhnath the most prominent of the Nath yogis, were responsible in reviving the ancient yogic teachings. The *Siddha Siddhanth Kaumudi*, the *Goraksha Shataka*, the *Gheranda Samhita*, the *Shiva Samhita*, the *Hathayoga Pradipika* are all works of Nath yogis and present the philosophical and practical aspects of yoga in a clear format.

M: Babaji, they say Yoga is derived from *Sankhya*. Will you please explain?

Babaji: *Sankhya*, which is one of the oldest *darshanas* (schools of philopsphy) of the Indian system of thought, is attributed to the great sage Kapila, who predates the *Puranas* and is also mentioned in the *Bhagavad Gita*, as the greatest of all sages. Now the *Sankhyas* are atheists like the Jains, and do not believe in a creator God. It is a dualistic philosophy in which *Purusha* which is pure consciousness is different from *Prakriti* which is matter. *Prakriti* or nature has its own laws and attributes and evolves according to the laws that govern its evolution. There is no greater God sitting and shaping things in his workshop. Nature functions according to cause and effect. *Prakriti* like *Purusha* is eternal and only keeps changing its state from one to another.

Now, *Purusha*, the pure spirit has become entangled with matter *Prakriti*. The process of spiritual evolution is the shedding of the binding factors of *Prakriti* and going back to the original state of pure consciousness. Even mind or thoughts, both according to yoga and *Sankhya*, is matter even at its subtlest levels and the aim of yoga is *Chitta Vriti Nirodha*, which is first restraining and then getting rid of the mind's activity, which is constantly engaged in various forms. A calm mind with no distractions and impurities when attained, intuitively understands the *Purusha* in its pristine, all pervading glory.

The Jain system of practice also has a similar background except that it believes in rigorous disciplining of the body and mind, verging on torture, so as to rise above the passions and desires and realize the bliss of resting in one's original self, free from all material conditions – *Nirvana*.

Yoga, however, does not agree with the adoption of extreme measures to bring about transformation and lays stress on moderation in everything: food, sleep and even meditation. From the philosophical point of view, there are very few differences between *Sankhya* and Yoga. The most important being that Patanjali admits is a personal God, *Ishwara* – not necessarily a creator God – but in the form of a first teacher. The only God that the Sankhyas admit is a nearly perfected being temporarily in charge of the spiritual evolution of a certain cycle of creation.

The other difference is that the yogis hold that the mind in its subtlest form is equally all pervading with the soul or *Purusha*. The *Sankhyas* do not agree with this. Be that as it may, both agree that the mind has to be freed of all distractions and opposites of attraction and repulsion, cleared of all violent thoughts and propensity for violent action and made quiet and tranquil, as a pre-requisite to the realization of the *Purusha*, which is pure consciousness, blissful and totally free.

The Jain *tirthankaras* have taught the same and apart from the extreme and torturous modus operandi, which yoga does not agree with, insist that the first rule to follow in the spiritual journey is complete non-violent *Ahimsa*; the first of rules (*yamas*) to be followed by the practising yogi according to the Yoga Sutras of Patanjali – practise non-violence in thought, word and deed, not causing injury to any living being.

M: Babaji, who can be called the greatest of Yogis?

Babaji: The great being called Krishna, who in the fifteenth chapter of the *Gita* calls himself *Purusha* of all excellences and who in the same *Gita* teaches a complete chapter on *Sankhya Yoga*, gives a concise description of the one he calls the "greatest of yogis". In the twelfth chapter, asked by his friend and disciple Arjuna to define the qualities of a great yogi, Krishna says:

one who is in control of his sense organs and emotions;

one who remains tranquil and equanimous in the midst of praise or blame, happiness or sorrow; and

175

one who is kind and compassionate and always thinks of the welfare of all living beings.

M: Babaji, do you mean to say that an atheist or an agnostic can practise yoga and attain the goal?

Babaji: There is no pre-condition to the practice of yoga, except that the atheist or the agnostic has to be convinced enough to follow the rules and regulations. After progressing and quietening the mind, the practioner based on his or her experiences, can decide the issue of God or no God. Even a person, who believes strongly in the existence of a God high up in heaven, leads a destructive life causing misery and sorrow to other living beings. I personally would not call such a person religious or a yogi.

A peaceful and compassionate atheist is better than a violent and cruel theist.

M: Babaji, will you recommend some books to be read by students interested in understanding yoga further?

Babaji: Yes, read the *Yoga Sutras* of Patanjali. Swami Vivekananda's commentary on the Yoga Sutras called *Raja Yoga* is a must. Also read the *Siddha Siddhantha Paddhati* and Svatmarama's *Hatha Yoga Pradipika*. You may also read the *Gheranda Samhita*. Another excellent commentary on the Yoga Sutras of Patanjali is the *Yoga Sudhakara* by the great Sadashiva Brahmendra.

Let me warn you – read but do not practise without guidance from a personal instructor for we are dealing with exact and precise techniques and one cannot afford wrong practice which may bring about negative effects.

Now go meditate son. Do your kriya and do the *Chakra Dharana* on your navel. Need a little bit of balancing there. *Alek Niranjan!*

Epilogue

IN THE CONCLUDING part of the first chapter of my autobiography *Apprenticed to a Himalayan Master*, I have said "...here is a story my Master told me...." I bring the entire story back to you once more. Now that you have read the rest of my memoirs, you'll probably understand the significance of the story. And so the journey continues.

* * * * *

Behind the famous temple of Badrinath, the sacred Himalayan shrine, which stands 13,000 feet above sea level, there exist a few large and small caves perched on top of nearly inaccessible cliffs. The temple is open to pilgrims only during the summer months. The rest of the year, the whole area is snow-bound. Even the Namboodiri priests from Kerala who have been officiating as priests since the time of Shankaracharya (a saint who renovated the temple hundreds of years ago and was himself from Kerala) go down to the village of Joshi Mutt and wait for the next pilgrim season. Only a few extraordinary beings continue to live and meditate in the caves even during winter.

A hundred years ago, one such extraordinary yogi sat in one of the caves, bare bodied except for his cotton loin cloth, absorbed in deep meditation on his inner self. He was fair and handsome with flowing black hair and a black beard, and while his eyes were closed, a peaceful smile lit his face as he enjoyed the inner joy of soul communion. This young yogi, who was just nineteen, came from a distinguished family of Vedic scholars from the holy city of Varanasi.

His ancestors had been disciples of a legendary yogi called Sri Guru Babaji, who it is believed has maintained his physical body in a youthful condition for many hundreds of years, even to this day.

This young man's father, himself a disciple of Babaji, had handed over his son to the great yogi at the tender age of nine. Since then he had wandered with his teacher (who had no fixed abode), the length and breadth of the Himalayas. A year ago, at the age of eighteen, he had graduated to the level of an independent yogi and since then had been wandering alone amongst the snow covered peaks of Kedar and Badri.

While our young yogi sat perfectly still in the yogic state called *samadhi*, a strange drama was unfolding before his closed eyes. Clawing his way up the steep, rocky ledge, an old man of the kind rarely seen in those parts pulled himself up on to the flat rock in front of the cave. His dirty green turban and soiled robe now almost torn to shreds, the rosary around his neck and his hennaed beard clearly indicated that he was a Muslim *fakir*.

There were cuts and bruises all over his arms, legs and other exposed parts of his body and blood oozed from his wounds. Cold and hungry, he was on the verge of collapsing, but as soon as his eyes fell upon the young yogi sitting in the cave, the pained expression on his face was replaced by a smile which expanded into hysteric laughter. "Praise be to Allah," he cried and with a deep sigh, forgetting all his pain and suffering, he moved towards the still meditating yogi and fell prostrate. He then did something no Hindu would ever dream of doing to a yogi – he hugged him.

The yogi, crudely shaken out of his trance, opened his eyes and shook off the old man who was clinging to his body. He blew his nose to clear the stench that came from the travel worn and bleeding body of the strange creature and shouted in anger, "How dare you? Keep away from me." Anger, that powerful poison that is sometimes difficult to control even for *rishis*, had entered this young yogi's heart.

"Please, Sir," pleaded the *fakir*, "Give me a chance to tell you my story." "Go away," said the yogi, "I need to have a dip in the Alakananda and resume my meditation. Your kind of person, a meat eating barbarian, has no place here. Get lost."

The *fakir* would not give up. "Please listen to me, O great yogi, I am a Sufi and am the chief disciple of a great Sufi master of the Naqshabandiya order. Just before my master passed away, six months ago, he told me, 'Friend, you have now reached the level of spiritual attainment that I was able to take you to. I am leaving my body soon and there is no Sufi master at this point who is willing to guide you to the next and higher level. But don't worry. There lives a young Himalayan yogi near Badri in the Himalayas. Find him and seek his help.' You are the one he referred to and you alone can save me now.

"For two months, I have suffered incalculable travails and misfortunes before finding you. I might drop dead due to exhaustion, but just accept me as your disciple and my soul will depart in peace. Please I beg you."

"I know nothing about your master or the Sufis as you call them. I have received no such instructions, and moreover, I don't accept disciples," said the young yogi still angry. "Now move out of my way and don't delay me from having my bath in the Alakananda and resume the meditation that you so rudely interrupted. Get out!"

"Alright, O great yogi," said the *fakir*, "if that is your final word, I don't wish to stay alive anymore. My life's only dream has been shattered. I shall jump into the river and take my life. May the Supreme Lord of the Universe guide me."

"Do what you want," said the yogi firmly, "but I can do nothing for you. You are lucky that, in my anger, I did not curse you. Go your way and let me go my way."

The *fakir* bade farewell by prostrating at the yogi's feet and with tears in his eyes, made his way to the river that flowed several feet below. With a prayer on his lips and seeking guidance from the Supreme Being, he plunged into the swirling waters and ended his life.

The young yogi, confident that he had done the right thing and having no remorse whatsoever, climbed down to a lovely spot on the banks of the river and, chanting the appropriate mantras for purification, had a dip in the extremely cold waters of the sacred river. He came out of the water and rubbed himself dry with the only towel that he possessed. Sitting on a rock, he thanked the sacred river for purifying his body and mind and was about to start his climb to the cave when he heard the familiar sweet voice of his master calling him, "Madhu!"

From behind a rocky ledge appeared his great master Babaji. It looked as if the darkness of the approaching dusk was suddenly lit by his glowing presence. Tall, fair with an almost European complexion, Babaji had long flowing brown hair and very little facial hair. He looked around sixteen years of age. The well-built unadorned muscular body was bare except for a white loin cloth. He was bare foot, and walked with great grace and dignity.

His large, meditative eyes fell on his young disciple Madhu. "What a terrible thing you have done my boy," he said softly.

Instantly, the gravity of what he had done a few minutes ago, hit him like lightning. "Babaji" was all he could utter before breaking into tears and prostrating at his feet.

"Control yourself my boy, and come. Let us climb up to your cave." They climbed up swiftly, reached the cave, and sat down facing each other. "Haven't I always told you to think before you speak about what you are going to say, to whom, and under what circumstances? You could have had a little more patience and listened carefully to what the old man was trying to say. Is a holy man judged by his outward appearance? Like my great disciple Kabir said, would you give more importance to the scabbard than to the sword? You have hurt and pained a great devotee of the Lord. All the fruits of your many years of austerities, you have destroyed in a flash. A minute of kindness is more precious than a hundred years of intense austerities. You have to compensate for it."

By then the young disciple had controlled himself and become calm. "Whatever you say, my Master, I am prepared to do," he said. "As for the *fakir*," said Babaji, "I shall take care of his spiritual needs. You have arrested your spiritual progress by your arrogant behaviour and the only way to get back on track is to go through the same or similar pain and privation that the *fakir* went through. Prepare to do the last *kriya* of total *khechari mudra* and let your *prana* exit through the *ajna* centre. We shall then guide your soul to be born in such circumstances that you go through pain similar to that suffered by the poor man. Do it now."

"Your wish has always been a command for me, Babaji, and I will do so immediately, but I have a last wish."

"Express it my son," said Babaji.

His voice breaking with deep emotion, and hands clasped in prayer, the young disciple said, "Master, I love you with all my heart. Promise that you will not let go of me, that you will keep track of me and not let me be carried away by the whirlpool of worldly thoughts and concerns. I beg you to please promise me that you will watch over me and bring me back to your blessed feet."

"That, I promise," said the great teacher, tender compassion tangibly flowing from his glittering eyes, "My foremost disciple, Maheshwarnath, whom you have not met, shall come to you quite early in your next life. He shall be your guide. At some point in your future life, you will also see me and talk to me as you are doing now. But now, you must hurry, for this is the right time to go."

By then, the sun had set and the beautiful silvery moon parted the clouds to bear witness to the sacred play that was being enacted. The young disciple, with tears in his eyes, prostrated once more at his guardian's feet. Babaji stretched forth his right hand, placed it on his head, blessed him and instantly merged into the night. Madhu, now alone, adopted the lotus posture, took a few deep breaths, performed the *khechari mudra* that forcibly stops the breathing process, and concentrating on the centre between the eyebrows, shook off his body.

That is the end of the story that my master Maheshwarnath told me.

Walk of Hope
Born Human be Human, Every Step for Humanity

On the 12th of January 2015, Sri M started on foot from Kanyakumari, the confluence of the three oceans. Accompanied by a large number of people he walked what he called 'The Walk of Hope' for Peace and Harmony, cutting across the heart of India for 7500 kms in roughly 500 days. In April 2016 the Walk entered Srinagar, Kashmir.

Sri M declared that the Walk was to sow the seeds of harmony and togetherness among human beings irrespective of caste, creed, religion and gender.

His talk to the Members of Parliament while in New Delhi, a transcript of which is given below, sums up the message of The Walk of Hope which Sri M undertook under the banner of The Manav Ekta Mission.

'Born Human be Human, Every Step for Humanity' was the slogan displayed on the white banner of Peace.

* * * * *

Sri M's Address to Members of the Parliament
Parliament House, New Delhi. 29 February 2016

First of all, my Namaskar, Salām Aleykum, Sat Sri Akaal and Good Evening to all.

Honourable Deputy Chairman of the Rajya Sabha Prof. P.J. Kurien, Sri Ravi Shankar Prasad, Honourable Minister

Sri M. Venkaiah Naidu, Honourable Minister Sri Mukhtar Abbas Naqvi, Honourable Minister of State Sri Suresh Prabhu, Honourable Minister Sri Manoj Sinha, Honourable Minister Sri Bandaru Dattatreya, Honourable Minister Sri Pon Radha krishnan, Honourable Minister of State Sri Dharam Vijay, Sri Oscar Fernandes who hails from my wife's native place in Udupi, and all honourable Members of Parliament, the *padyatris* (walkers) who are here, ladies and gentlemen and members of the media.

I will start my talk with a Sanskrit *shloka* (verse) that is 3000 years old. As I am from the South, please excuse my Hindi:

Sarve Bhavantu Sukhinah
Sarve Santu Niraamayaah,
Sarve Bhadraanni Pashyantu
Maa Kashcid Dukha Bhaag Bhavet
Lokaah Samastaah Sukhino Bhavantu

Just because this verse is in Sanskrit, please do not assume that it belongs to any particular caste or creed or religion. This is a universal saying. These days, if we say something in Sanskrit, it is assumed to belong to a particular set of people and, if you say something in Arabic, then it is assumed that it belongs to some other set. The meaning of this verse is:

May all become happy, May all be free from illness.
May all see what is Auspicious, May no one have *dukha* (suffering)
May the entire universe be in *sukha* (happiness).

This walk was started in Kanyakumari on the 12th of January 2015. Why Kanyakumari? Kanyakumari marks the confluence of three seas. Since this Walk is one of coalescence and about bringing people together – although we are already united and are one, we tend to fall apart sometimes – we felt a *sangam* (confluence) would be a good choice to start our Walk from.

A second reason for us to choose Kanyakumari was that 12th January is the birth anniversary of Swami Vivekananda. The spiritual work he did a hundred years ago for *Manav Ekta* (human solidarity) cannot be done by a thousand people in a hundred years. Swami Vivekananda roamed around India as a *parivrajaka* (a wandering renunciant). Having wandered around the country, he reached Kanyakumari, where there was nothing but a cliff in the middle of the sea. He swam across the sea and meditated on that cliff for three days, after which he understood the work he was supposed to do thereafter. So, we thought that this place and date would be appropriate to start this Walk.

We have walked around 5800 kms so far. I am not alone. With me are 60 to 70 people – whom we call the core group – who are walking with me from Kanyakumari. These people belong to different states, different sects, different religions and we all are walking together. And, after walking this much, I am happy to tell you that India's *Manav Ekta* is still intact.

The question that arises then is – "Why then are you walking? If everything is set, why are you doing this?"

When we started from Kanyakumari, we had a very good response. When we reached Kerala, we had a much bigger response. I thought this might be because it is my home state. But, when we went to the next state, the response was much better. More people started coming. We completed one year in Kanpur on the 12th of January this year. There was an overwhelming response. Now we have come to Delhi. I think some effect has taken place definitely without which I wouldn't even have had the privilege of getting invited to the Parliament annex to address the MPs. We still have almost another 2000 kms to walk. We intend to reach Srinagar on the 1st of May. As I said, people ask "If there is *Manav Ekta*, then what are you doing for it?" Yes there is unity amongst us but, sometimes, it starts fraying. And once the breakdown rises, it can get out of hand.

There is no other nation in the whole world like ours – with 22-23 languages, so many religions, so many sects, so many ideologies from left to right and centre. In spite of all this, an average citizen will call himself a Hindustani, a *Bharatvasi*, an Indian. No one will say otherwise. But sometimes, one sees that this unity starts to rupture, and when that happens, the fire that rages with it cannot be extinguished even with water. We felt these communal riots or ideological or political problems are a facade to conceal someone's vested interest.

We have been to small villages, to the interiors, where – in a majority community of a thousand people – there are three Muslim families or two Christian families and they all live together without any problem. There are places like these which we have visited and when we talked to them, they said that such incidents (of disunity) do occur sometimes. When asked why, they told us to look carefully and added that the issue would reveal itself to be the self-interest of somebody else.

We thought that this unity needs to be maintained and not broken. It is customary in India to live together as one. It is in our *Samskar* (tradition) and it is not something new. As is written in Rig Veda:

"sangacchadhvam"
Let's walk together
"samvadadhvam"
Let's talk together
"samvo manaamsi jaanatam"
Let's bring our minds together to understand

As Prof. Kurien said: *"Ekam sat vipraa bahudaa vadanti"*, the meaning of which everyone knows. I once went to a University in America and a professor there began his lecture with the same shloka, Ekam sat vipraa bahudaa vadanti.

We tell everyone we meet that our country being a democracy, ideological differences and differences of opinion will exist. Otherwise, this can't be a democracy. But despite the differences, we are first of all *manav* (human). We are, first and foremost, *manushya* (human). Everybody is born from a mother's womb. No one falls from the sky. And when the time comes, it is unto this earth we all go, whether it is a *kabristan* (cemetery) or a *smashan* (crematorium). Why can't we play this small drama between birth and death in peace and harmony? I thought this is possible and this was the first thing we needed to convey.

The second thing was whatever our faith and ideology, we always need to remember that we are Indians first. This ancient land, which has seen many *rishis* (sages), welcomed so many religions. Whoever came was never refused. That this land is ours and we are its citizens is something we should always remember.

191

These are the two things that we are trying to make people understand. And I am happy to say that people listen to this and understand it. They say they will not let any untoward incident happen again. This is not curative but a preventive measure. When someone falls sick and goes to the hospital to get medicine, he either dies or survives. But, if inoculated beforehand for the disease, the person wouldn't fall sick in the first place. That is the best course of action.

We talk to people about prevention and tell them to not let these incidents happen in the first place and stay united. But if tendencies do crop up due to someone's greed and vested interests, that would be the time to tell those who are responsible, 'We have heard you out but we don't support it, so please end it here. We will not let violence take place and we will not fall apart either.'

It is my experience that a small spark of Divinity resides in all hearts. In Sufism, it is called 'Khuda ka Noor'. This Atman (spirit) or ansh (portion) is present in all. This would mean that each one of us is a moving temple or a mosque. The aradhana or worship of these moving temples is not through arti (ritual worship) but through seva (service). Swami Vivekananda used to always say: Atmano mokshartham jagat hitaaya cha meaning (each one's life is) "For one's own salvation and for the welfare of the world". That is an individual's journey. But the welfare of the world is the duty of all. Since this is my experience, I cannot deny it. Be it Amar, Akbar or Anthony – whichever ideology one chooses – we are one and the same. In Kerala, where I come from, there are also ideologies which do not believe in the existence of God. That is fine too, as long as they believe in humanity and don't hurt anybody and live happily together.

I go to schools and colleges to educate the students about this. Our generation might have committed some mistakes – mistakes that can be avoided in the future. We have met thousands of students and in their hearts we have sown the seeds of humanity. We have also taught them that we are the citizens of this country and we will hold steady against any outward or inward negative influences without falling apart. This is what we have said along the way. When we sow seeds, they do not sprout the next day. It takes time. To nurture these seeds is the responsibility of parents and teachers, and you (the politicians) too. The politicians should think a little bit more about this and try to keep the country together for we are all one. Those in power can do much more than what we, the general public, can. I was happy to be invited and come here as it gave me an opportunity to talk with you about this.

I have full faith that the seeds we sow today will grow up into trees, under whose shade we would be able to live peacefully and harmoniously. This is my wish and my prayer. Even if a country is economically secure, without peace it won't mean anything. Peace, Harmony and Human Oneness are of utmost importance. United we stand, divided we fall.

It is a privilege to stand before you, this August assembly, and share my thoughts with you. I have to thank Sri Pon Radhakrishnan, Minister of State. The moment we told him that this *yatra* (journey) is to start from Kanyakumari, he asked us to start from Zero Point, and allotted the land there.

We have got help from various quarters. You have seen the film on how we have interacted with Chief Ministers, cutting across political barriers. You know that while politics is important, we are a democracy. There will be differences of opinion but – in the heart of hearts – all of us know that we are human beings and we have to live together and make this nation great. It is already a great nation but can we come together and ensure that it becomes much more glorious than it was or is? Let us not just think about past glories and forget the present. Let's move forward for a bright future. This is my earnest request and prayer.

I know all of you cannot walk with us but if you support us with your minds, our Walk will accomplish its objectives much before we reach Srinagar in Kashmir. So, once more, I thank you and pray that you are with us.

Thank you. Namaskar.

*Walk begins
at Kanyaku-
mari*

*Walk of Hope
in Bangalore
city*

International Summit on Peace and Harmony, Varanasi

Sri Vishwambarnath Mishra, Mahant, Sankat Mochan Foundation with Mr Adama Dieng of the UN and Sri M at Tulsidas Ghat, Varanasi, Uttar Pradesh

Spiritual luminaries on stage at Siri Fort Auditorium, Delhi

2

Celebration of Hope with Indian Ocean in Nehru Park New Delhi

Addressing youth in Delhi

A selfie with students

3

Chief Minister of Karnataka, Sri Siddarama-iah at the Walk

Walk of Hope at the banks of Ganga, Allahabad

Offering aarti to River Kaveri at Bhagamandala in Karnataka.

Dialogue of Hope in Karnataka as part of the Walk

Reception at Khatabillod, Dhar district, Madhya Pradesh

Reception by Anganavadi workers at Kandhiya village in U P

Walk of Hope reaches Srinagar, Kashmir

With the Prime Minister of India, Sri Narendra Modi

With the President of India, Sri Pranab Mukherjee

7

With the Former President of India, late Dr. A. P. J. Abdul Kalam

With Smt Sonia Gandhi and Sri Rahul Gandhi

With His Holiness The Dalai Lama

With His Holiness Pope Francis at Vatican in Rome

With His Holiness Dr. Shivamurthy Shivacharya Mahaswamiji, Seer of Taralabalu Jagadguru Brihanmath, Sirigere, Karnataka

With social reformer Sri Anna Hazare

With Arch Bishop George Alencherry, Catholic Cardinal

With actor Sri Rajani Kant

At Sri Harmandir Sahib 'Golden Temple', Amritsar

At the Triveni Sangam in Kanyakumari before the Walk of Hope started

Chief Minister of Kerala Sri Pinarayi Vijayan and Former Chief Minister Sri Oommen Chandy

With Rashtriya Swayamsevak Sangh Sarsanghchalak Sri Mohan Bhagwat ji.

With Sri Suresh Bhaiyya Ji Joshi, Sarkaryawaha - Rashtriya Swayamsevak Sangh(RSS)

With Union Minister Sri R avishankar Prasad, Dr. Najma A. Heptulla and Prof P. J. Kurien, Deputy Speaker of Rajya Sabha

Sri M welcoming Sardar Anwar Hussain Kazmi Chishty, Gaddanashin, Aulia Masjid, Dargah Sharif, Ajmer

Sri M. N. Venkatachaliah, Former Chief Justice of India and Dr. Karan Singh, Member of Parliament

Addressing the Members of Parliament in Delhi during the Walk of Hope

Prof. P.J. Kurien and Sri Shashi Tharoor during Nirahar Sat yagraha at Jantar Mantar, Delhi held during the Walk of Hope

With K.S. Puttannaiah, farmer leader in Karnataka